THE PSYCHOLOGY
OF THE
SCHOOL-AGE CHILD

CONTENTS

INTRODUCTION

Nowadays, our ears ring with semi-scandalous and pitiable tales of ill-reared children and supposedly "impossible brats." It is certain that education has for some years now become far from something simple: recent disturbances, long absences, all the difficulties of modern life have not helped parents in their task of rearing souls. These few pages are intended to aid them as well as all teachers who bear this magnificent charge.

The very frequent failures of present-day education are certainly the result in great part of the harmful pressures of a social environment more or less convulsed by war and its consequences; but we must also realize that just as great a part in these failures is owed to the flagrant unpreparedness of teachers for their role which has now become delicate.

Too often we harbor a profound ignorance concerning the nature and needs of the child. For no one has taken the trouble to prepare us for this difficult task and in particular to help us understand our children better. We have a poor understanding of the child because it is not easy to grasp his mentality. He expresses himself very badly; and if we often mitigate his inadequacies of language by "reading on his face" the emotions he is experiencing, how often are we deceived concerning what he wishes to hide from us! What is more, the child does not always give words the same meaning we do: he sees *absolutes* where our indulgence sees only the *relative,* and he does not really understand that a law obliges him as a child but does not always oblige his parents or companions. What sources of incomprehension and shock lie therein, and who could boast at having always understood the jargon of the child?

The child is misunderstood by us because he is much different from us. It has been the common belief for a long time—and if one has not thought it, one has behaved in this respect as if one thought it—that the child is a man in miniature, one "less capable," someone similar to us but less developed. We will see that this entirely false conception is at the root of a good many misunderstandings.

We might note in passing two examples of these differences of mental attitudes between the child and ourselves:

His vision of the world is fragmentary, never panoramic: the child of Duhamel,[1] brought to the circus for the first time, notices the elephant dung in the middle of the floor and fails to remember the spectacle itself.

He reasons in a way that seems absurd to us. A test of Piaget concerning the notion of space can provide us with one example among a thousand others: we place two cubes (or any other objects) on a table at some distance from each other. Then we interpose

---

[1] G. Duhamel, *Les plaisirs et les jeux* (Mercure de France).

a bulky object (small box, stack of books) and ask the child: "Is the distance between the cubes less or greater when we interpose the box or when we remove it?" Until the child reaches the neighborhood of seven, he invariably replies that the distance is less when the box is present.

What separates the child and adult mentalities is not a simple difference of degree or maturation; it is a profound difference of nature. For each stage of child development possesses its own psychological originality, for the most part irreducible to adult psychology. Some of these radical differences will be seen throughout this book.

Knowledge of those we work with

It is not enough for an engineer to know his formulas; he must also know the workers he employs. The family doctor and the spiritual director who know their clients provide better treatment and direction than the first doctor who comes along and a random priest in the confessional. Just as the cultivator knows his land and the sculptor knows the grain of his marble, just as the builder knows not only his tools but the material he uses, so must we who are teachers know our children. We will act ineffectually *on* the child to help him grow and develop and *with* the child to enable him to radiate an apostolic faith unless we are thoroughly familiar not only with the techniques and materials to be used but above all with the child himself in his complexity and simplicity, refashioning in ourselves a childlike attitude in order to accompany him toward a full adult life.

Otherwise, if you plan—for his sake—to draw upon the remembrances of your distant childhood, you will only drag out a lot of old ideas distorted by an adult view and you will be doomed to failure.

If you regard your intuition as prophetic and your cleverness as infallible, you are in trouble; for without humility you cannot get inside the mind of a child, and you will be doomed to failure.

If you regard your influence as overwhelming and the prestige of your thirty years, your male voice, or your teaching chair as sovereign, forget such ideas. Ask God to inspire in you greater respect for the freedom he has given to this emerging personality: become children yourselves among children.

And if fear of the "ridiculous" holds you back from regarding their lives and pains, their joys and labors, from the child's viewpoint which sees all things in proportion to the measure of their powers, then believe me your place is not with these little ones; your old-fashioned attitude will crush them and squeeze the life out of them!

Yet we could make no graver error than to consider the task easy: it is worthwhile for us to contribute all our powers and our whole heart to it, for it is a grand and noble task.

Two ways of regarding the child

1. Comparison of the child with the adult

We will thus make a certain number of observations concerning the profound nature of the child, which is so different from our own. His essential characteristics will be underlined: activity, egocentrism, etc. We call this the *static aspect* of the psychology of the child.

2. Comparison of the child with himself

This involves comparing the stages of the child's evolution and examining the continual growth of functions in his physical, mental and social existence. We will thus distinguish three major periods of growth, separated by periods of crisis which normally manifest themselves in all children. This is the *genetic aspect* of the psychology of the child.

These two methods, treated successively, will lead us to a better definition of the psychological structure of the child. They complete each other. We will begin with the static aspect which by characterizing the child as a whole from his first few months until adolescence will help us in the genetic study of his mental faculties.

PART ONE

GENERAL CHARACTERISTICS OF THE CHILD IN COMPARISON WITH ADULTS

A CONSTANTLY IMPROVING BEING

What immediately strikes us about the child and dominates his entire psychology from birth to maturity is first and foremost the enormous *power of adaptation* of his whole being.

There is the *physical* adaptation of a body in full development: growth is only a maturation of organs which renders them ever more suitable for their function. The example of the long evolution of the nervous system which remains still indeterminate at birth, until its effective completion at puberty, is striking. The evolution of the digestive tract which transforms and adapts itself in a few years from the mother's milk to store meat is just as remarkable.

There is also the *mental* adaptation of a mind at first totally isolated in an unknown world, gradually discovering its surroundings, utilizing in ever better fashion the data of the senses (which are being refined) and recomposing them later into intellectual edifices oriented for the most part toward adapting the child to the exterior world. The slow evolution of the individual's means of knowing is in short intended only to enable him to go through life without bruises and without danger.

There is, finally, a *social* adaptation of a personality which is seeking itself and finds itself through sudden jolts by more or less violently opposing those around it and which will achieve its autonomy as a man only at the price of these battles. This represents a considerable adaptation on the part of a being who at its beginnings is nothing more than dependence and passivity and yet becomes—in the midst of a social world gradually enlarged from the cradle to adult human framework—an active and free cog of a society in which he must live and work.

There is something grand and infinitely respectable in this vital force, this tendency toward progress, this enormous power of perfectibility which is the precious hallmark of childhood and youth: the person who is no longer adaptable is already old.

This entails a *great duty of trust and respect* on the part of an adult and a teacher in particular. Respect for the personality which is being constructed in order eventually to serve God and its brothers. Respect for this force directed toward the good and the better! Woe to the blasé adult who stifles this force; and this is the terrible responsibility borne by the circle of a good many children in whom this flame of generosity and ardor was unable to be preserved.

We must respect this power for progress which will decrease ever so quickly, and try to resurrect it in us if we have had the misfortune to neglect it: our task as teachers on behalf of the child's progress is not possible without our own progress.

One form of this respect is to *take the child seriously*. His efforts, successes and failures, his joys and sorrows, his work and play—all is in accord with his powers: these are not trifles, insignificant baubles, puerile and negligible. They are meritorious efforts, ending in huge successes or dismal failures; the child may possibly rise more swiftly from them than we from ours, but they still weigh very heavily on his daily life just as our efforts, pains and joys weigh on our own adult lives.

We must try not to let the child avoid these daily experiences with their happiness and misfortunes: it is this perpetual contact with reality which will forge a vigorous personality. *Overly sheltered children* have not had these experiences and *will not know how to behave as adults* in the hard life that awaits them. We must also take care not to make this burden heavier by our adult concerns which should not weigh upon the child: wait till he is at school or in bed at night before discussing the thorny problem of the family budget. The child should indeed be aware of our efforts to assure him a full life, but these efforts should weigh on us and not on him!

In short, we must render to the experiences undergone by the child on contact with the exterior world all the importance they merit—and nothing more. We must take at its face value (which is great) this training in life acquired by the child little by little in accord with his powers, and not overburden him with premature cares and efforts.

(For greater clarity we will set off—at irregular intervals and on separate pages—some practical conclusions that can be drawn from what has gone before.)

The Fine Art of Teaching

To oblige a child to remain motionless and mute for ten or fifteen minutes is almost as contrary to his nature and as tiring for him, as to oblige him to walk and hop on one leg at the same time.

Are your children unnerving? Do not yell at them to be quiet and remain tranquil, but let them shout and gesticulate for a moment. You will then have no trouble in gently calming them by means of some activity they like.

If there are sparks in the air and we feel an argument brewing, we must not wait till it has already erupted but direct it ourselves. If we take the initiative, everything will turn out well. If the students do so, be prepared for trouble!

As for those of you who are heads of families, I can well understand that you may be tired from your work by evening and wish to read your paper. However, do not forget that the children also have a wish, which for them is an absolute necessity, to move about after their immobility at school. You are therefore faced with one of two solutions: flight or courage.

For my part, I prefer the second for several reasons: to know how to play with a child is to gain his confidence (I will need this so much when he is fifteen!) You can read your paper when they are in bed; in fact, it will be a good reason for you to send them to bed earlier and for them to get their full share of sleep.

ACTIVITY AND RECEPTIVITY

This vital force is manifested principally by two sets of closely connected functions: the functions of receptivity or passivity, and the functions of restitution or activity.

The child is *essentially an active being,* constantly developing, continually in motion. He needs a good deal more calories than an adult (in proportion to their respective weights). A child who is excessively calm, too smart or not exuberant enough is very disquieting: this is generally the sign of an organism which is in danger; it indicates old age before its time.

The child is also a *receptive being,* open and penetrable; we are thinking of the enormous sum of acquisitions between birth and adulthood, of the multiple learning processes which he must experience; some are very complicated, as for example, that of language. No adult could ever do the same! Witness our difficulty in assimilating a foreign language. Learning to walk or to see on the part of adults who have never walked or seen is a very lengthy process and never so perfect or so sure as in the case of children.

1. Corporal activity

The child requires motion to exercise his muscles, strengthen his bony frame, enrich his blood, develop his lungs and refine his nervous system. Exercise is as indispensable for him as nourishment. It is one of the major errors of school, as it is still conceived in too many places, to force the child to remain still while niggardly granting him a few quarter hours of recreation (perhaps only after he has been freed from "standing in the corner" because he has been too fidgety in class—which is just the opposite of what simple common sense would dictate!).

Not only is motion necessary for the child's development; it also represents an indispensable safety value for the excess of nervous energy accumulated during his periods of immobility. There are of course other safety valves! But you can guess what they are, and it is best to avoid them: the child's excessive nervousness will suddenly break out in violent movements, in uncontrollable crying or laughter, and in unbridled rows.

2. Sensorial receptivity

It is sufficient merely to observe the child's face to realize at once the avidity of his senses: his mouth half open ready to absorb or suck, his nostrils flaring to the wind, his eyes opened wide upon the world and watching all that is taking place. See his ears like "cabbage leaves" also alert to the sounds all about them: what *openness* this all entails!

On the other hand, let us look at the "uncommunicative" or "closed" child: his mouth is shut, his nostrils a little more pinched, his eyes half-hidden by the lids and the puckered eyebrows. The child who is

19

no longer in a receptive state is as disquieting as the child who is not active. His intellectual development will feel the effects.

This wide extent of "openness" on the part of the normal child and his great sensorial receptivity explain one of the most striking features of the child and one of the most useful for the teacher to know: the child is almost exclusively *permeable by the concrete,* by what he sees, hears, touches and handles. Thus this extraordinarily live curiosity manifests itself by the need to touch everything, to take apart "in order to see how something is made" and by the incessant "why." Yet he attaches less importance to the answers than to his own experiences.[2]

The curiosity of the child, who "sticks his nose into everything," is one of his riches: it enables him to discover the whole world around him in a few years' time. But unfortunately it is something which is often stamped out by the school with its bookish procedures, its omnibus programs, and its aversion for whatever is not in accord with traditional exercises.

School still remains much too intellectual and for this reason wastes the child's time, energies and interest. The child who at seven or eight years of age was still curious, inquisitive and full of imagination gradually loses all desire to know and seek things out for himself. We then come upon fifteen-year-olds who no longer read anything but mysteries and do not care to extend their knowledge because they are no longer curious about anything!

---

[2] Until he is almost eight years old, the child is incapable of entering into the thought of another in order to understand most of these answers. Thus the questions *(which must nevertheless be answered)* often have merely the value of a monologue.

Everything has its own time! Until he is ten, the child has no need of manuals but of concrete objects; when ideas become accessible to him at ten or twelve, we can then envisage progressive change of method.

The Fine Art of Teaching

Be concerned if you encounter a child who is not curious, just as you must be concerned about a child who is too intelligent. Call on your ingenuity to provide him with interesting occupations. Only through interest (not through obligation) will you be able to overcome what you look upon as laziness.

Laziness, excessive wisdom and lack of curiosity are three allied sicknesses that must be treated in analogous fashion. I call them sicknesses rightly. I know of no honest doctor who treats a sickness with slaps or punitive chores. But I know many good people who treat their children's laziness in such manner!

As for intelligence in a child, how many rejoice in it and congratulate themselves over it when often they should be concerned about it! Concerned about an excessive intelligence, at least.

These three sicknesses of the child could have a thousand different and mixed origins: physical deficiency (nervous, glandular or even intestinal), myopia or partial deafness, teachers who do not give enough encouragement, jealousies among children, fatigue resulting from the growing process, emotional shocks from a harmful atmosphere, etc. So many reasons which are not taken care of by raps of rulers on the knuckles!

Whenever it is possible to impart knowledge by showing an object, having it passed from hand to hand, touched, handled, returned, drawn, weighed, compared and broken—do so. If you do not have the object, let your children look for it in nature, in the street, at the market or in the museum. If this is not possible, help them find a large, clear and distinct picture which represents the object under its various aspects.

And if it is still not to be found, as a last resort, take if you will a good description in a manual and comment on it; but then, believe me, this will represent a lot of time lost!

3. Mental activity

The child's body is not the only thing in motion. His spirit is too! The materials streaming in through his senses are largely utilized. If he does not yet know how to arrange them (for, as we shall see, his observations are fragmentary) in unconscious syntheses as the adult does, at least he utilizes them willingly. His imagination is lively and his games are filled with picturesque embellishments.

We must note, however, that the imagination undergoes a partial eclipse between the ages of nine and thirteen owing in great part—as we have mentioned —to the rigidity of traditional school exercises. On the one hand, these do not provide enough concrete materials for the child's mind so that he can use them to create new things and, on the other, they leave no room for fantasy, do not allow personal freedom and force all the children into the same mold. School destroys spontaneity by the passivity of its methods.

This serious reproach and various others which we will make later are directed not at the school itself but at the methods it employs. Wherever teaching has boldly freed itself from traditional passive methods and brought into play the whole personality of the child through *active methods,* the child has gone on to develop much more and the educative result has been heightened sooner or later by his full voluntary participation in the efforts of his teachers.[3]

We should also note, on the subject of imagination, that between the ages of four and eight the child readily lives the wondrous deeds he fashions for him-

---

[3] Another deformation effected by the school is that through its *passive discipline* it forces the child to be the enemy of the teacher and to accept more or less the opposite of what he says! Still, the child unknowingly remains all the same strongly marked by his teacher's ideas.

self, poorly distinguishing the frontiers of the real and the imaginary. At puberty, on the contrary, he will readily take refuge in his dreams knowing when to leave them and when to reenter them, to forget the world around him and the past which he repudiates.

4. Mental receptivity

Through the vestibules of his largely opened senses, the child also embraces the ideas proposed to him by adults, books or things, and the answers to his countless questions. His spirit is profoundly disposed to believe whatever one tells him.

We should therefore respect his credulity. The child is eminently suggestible and this is a very useful factor in education. The child will have the same opinion of himself that his teachers have; and if they do not believe in his capacities, if they do not from time to time affirm his true talents (there are always at least one or two!), he will quickly be convinced without saying anything that he is good merely for using the bottom of his britches.

He will attribute to things whatever importance his teachers give them. He will accept with the same facility the most diverse opinions and unknowingly imitate the attitudes of those he encounters. School education cannot be neutral: a teacher influences his entire class by his simple attitude of neutrality and roots in the child's mind the idea that one can live without personal opinion and without a higher ideal. The child is a more or less conscious imitator. Attention should be given to the great power of example, good or bad.

The Fine Art of Teaching

The child is suggestible; hence do not tell him at every moment that he is stupid and good for nothing, a loafer and other pleasantries. First of all, the child has a right to politeness. Secondly, if you are impolite to him, he will be impolite to others and, behind your back, to you. Finally, he will be stricken by what you say and will be even more stupid and good for nothing to the extent that you have riveted the idea in his head!

The child is suggestible; hence, do not place him in a bad category, for then he will be bad toward you. Do not label him as slovenly, for he will then be slovenly in everything. Place him in a clear, gay and clean locale and sing with him.

The child is suggestible; hence, do not forget that you have before you as many mirrors as there are faces. If you are a sourpuss, you will certainly get thirty sourpusses back; and if you do not radiate much love, you will get back only indifference.

But if you wear your joy on your face, you will see thirty smiles before you, and your burden will be lighter, and so will that of their parents. Go ahead then and sow smiles; you will reap a hundred for each one.

The child is suggestible and credulous; hence, never make fun of him and do not use irony, for he takes everything seriously and you will only sow discouragement, bitterness and even hatred. I am not exaggerating in the least!

5. Very lively feelings

At once passive and active, the child's feelings run deep. He has a more or less conscious need for affection which is very great; if this need is not even moderately satisfied, the child will shut himself off, wither away and enter egoistically into himself. The child is not open only to sensorial impressions; he is also open to sympathy. He needs love as much as he needs fresh air.

Under another aspect, we must say that the child's sensitivity is acute. His feelings are as violent as they are short-lived. He is as profoundly loving as he is hostile. He is emotional and exuberant.

6. Conclusion

In the psychological characteristics we have just described we can observe a nice balance between passivity and activity. The child is passive and receptive by his senses, his credulity and his emotionality. He is active by his agitated body, his curious, inquisitive and imaginative nature, and his exuberant feelings.

It is the vigor of this current of exchanges which characterizes childhood and youth. Old age is a physical and intellectual egoism which rejects corporal and mental effort as well as expansion and reception. Until the end of adolescence, the miniature man is total abandonment and total generosity because he is filled with riches; he gives himself without counting the cost because he receives in abundance.

There is a vital need for a balance between these two tendencies to avoid the poor development of the child; it must be safeguarded to prevent disorders or permanent mental poverty.

The healthy child, physically as well as mentally,

is a being who receives and gives, who absorbs and gives out;[4] one who is gracious (receptive) and generous (giving).

Finally, we must insist upon the *absolute necessity,* on the one hand, of *allowing the child* this corporal, mental and emotional *activity:* that he might have someone to love, some time to dream and invent and some place to run and shout. And, on the other hand, there is just as much necessity to leave to the capacity of the child what is needed for his corporal, mental and emotional nourishment *(to allow the child this receptivity),* that is, that he might be loved as he deserves, that he find food for his curiosity and experiences just as much as he receives food for his body.

Functional exercise, that is, the gratuitous and non-obligatory exercise of each of his corporal and mental possibilities, remains the inescapable condition for the orderly functioning of all the child's movements.

It is the task of *games* to put all the child's faculties to work. They provide indispensable exercise for his body and needed training for his muscles which attain strength and suppleness, his physique which acquires solidity and his nervous reflexes which become rapid, precise and effective only to the extent that he uses them frequently at play. The apathetic child is the poorest, the most desperate and the least educable of children simply because of the poverty of his exchanges (reception-restitution) with the external world.

The same holds true for his other faculties; his will and determination can become real only through

---

[4] A child stricken with chronic constipation gradually shuts himself off from life. Observe his closed eyes and mouth. He is less personable. His sympathy is no longer ready for the first one to appear. The equilibrium is broken: mental and physical receptivity and activity diminish simultaneously.

gratuitous, disinterested exercise not directed toward a paying object. His intellectual faculties: memory, imagination, modes of knowing and elaboration, will become accomplished only through frequent use. The child really understands only what he does, only what he lives: playing is all of this; it is the right fuel for his spirit. Teachers should be aware of this fact and draw the proper conclusions.

The Fine Art of Teaching

We want this child to sprout straight for the sky like some vigorous fir-tree from our mountains. We must then ourselves be scrupulously loyal and honest, making certain that our moral law and his coincide and that our way is not devious and twisted. Exceptions and extenuating circumstances represent scandals in the child's eyes. War with its necessary compromises has amply demonstrated this. Our casuistry should be directed only at other knavish adults. For the child, only one way is possible—the most honest and the most just.

A sincere and bright smile, a heart which does not shrink from effort and a continual concern to help and serve: these three factors include everything. As far as means are concerned, and laws, commandments, precepts and usages, must we be concerned about them? We would do well to stick to the three factors and to nothing but them: the rest will come as surplus.

We must not require thirty-six things at once from a child. These three suffice: (1) that he always looks you straight in the eye when he speaks: you will then know when his spirit is sick and be able to heal it; (2) that he never says no to any task before he has loyally tried it: he will soon be stronger and bolder than you; (3) and that his ambition is to serve to the very last: he will grow in all respects by giving himself completely.

We must patiently seek the way in which we might reach the child who appears insensitive and above all never strike him. Our blows will only make his spirit which is already turned in on itself become ever more closed. We must confidently give him little things to do in keeping with his capacity. This will be more effective than our punishments in slowly educating his weakened moral sense.

CONSEQUENCES

This activity and receptivity have numerous profound consequences with respect to the child, among which we will distinguish principally the following.

1. In the order of the will, the child is incapable of inhibition.

He cannot control his vital force voluntarily; he cannot control his spontaneity. The child is no more capable of controlling the suggestions of his imagination than those he receives from those about him.

We must at least make sure that these suggestions are not negative. Rather than give him negative orders that he has trouble following ("don't slouch"; "don't make any noise") we should encourage him to follow our positive counsels and affirmative slogans ("a real boy is always loyal"; "say 'good morning' with a smile"). Certain ways of giving orders provoke disobedience!

Collective or social sports, through their rules and ruses, will be an excellent way for the ten- or twelve-year-old slowly to master his impulsiveness and attain the mastery which he lacks.

2. *In the order of intelligence, the child has ways of thinking which are very different from ours.*

A. His vision of things is never panoramic but latches on to a detail which strikes him and which he does not know how to connect with the whole. He is fascinated by the color of the feather on a lady's hat without remembering the shape of the hat or still less the lady beneath it!

B. His memory suffers the consequences. It forms a curious assortment of odd details along the lines of the contents of his pockets. These are all inadequately related, not arranged in harmonious syntheses like those which will please his masculine spirit later on.

C. His reasoning is not yet formed. He is incapable of deduction (going from a general principle to the particular conclusion) and induction (going from concrete particular cases to the abstract general principle). His thinking works by analogy; one of his preferred sayings is: "It's like." He will say, for example, "A pit in a fruit is like a stone in the woods." "A pen nib is like a poplar."

All of this baffles our adult outlook; the child sometimes puts so much fantasy in his odd associations that all logic is excluded—at least our kind of logic! He associates details without being able to see a wider scheme of things.

The source of this apparent incoherence is really the child's great permeability to the concrete data of the senses and his incapacity to handle abstract ideas: receiving a considerable quantity of sensorial impressions at each instant, he accumulates them for better or worse as randomly as he encounters them. It is only through a very *long labor of the unconscious* that these data gradually become associated through proximity (he also utilizes them in the play of his imagination) but still without logical connection.

Why then do we labor to put into his head lofty abstract principles (catechetical formulas, for instance), when he can retain only precise and lived details (visible deeds of charity, living teachings of a Gospel translated into modern language)?

3. In the order of emotion and intelligence, the child is egocentric.

This is not to say that he refers everything consciously back to himself (egoism), *but that he thinks and acts as if he were the center of the world:* egocentrism.

This tendency is natural, spontaneous and explicable: he would never have taken his first steps in the learning process except with this tendency as a basis, isolated as he was in his powerlessness as a newborn. He has gradually discovered the adult world in widening concentric circles about himself; this is true of the intellectual level.

On the emotional level, he has been accustomed from the beginning to be served, to receive the affection of his parents simultaneously with their care; hence, the emotional shock upon the birth of a small brother: "Mom, give my little brother to the lady," and the jealousy of the firstborn.

All this explains why the child naturally considers himself as the center of all that exists, and that the world gravitates around him, at his service. Rising progressively from his isolation as a newborn, the child discovers the world first in the aspects which interest him, which concern him personally. The child's own person is the prop for his first construction of the world. Long years of childhood will be needed before he is capable of grasping the more or less abstract relations uniting things, persons and himself.

A striking illustration of this attitude is that of the child under seven who volunteers a definition for everything based on usage: "The sun *exists to* give *us* light"; "the river *exists for us* to go boating." The whole world has been created for the child for the sole purpose of serving him (universal finalism).

Here is another example of egocentrism: total lack of concern to make himself understood characterizes the words of the child until about the age of six or seven. When he narrates, he speaks as if for himself, without imagining that somebody else might not understand him, and without entering sufficiently into the thinking of others (until about nine or ten years of age) to adapt his proper language to it; in short, without sufficient relations.

There is nothing in the least abnormal about this: it would be as absurd and unnatural to blame a child for his manifestations of egocentrism as to blame him for his shortness, or to reproach him for badly digesting spicy foods! It is absolutely necessary for the better understanding of the child that the adult refuse once and for all to regard this egocentrism as blameworthy and reprehensible.

At the beginning of his life the child is in such a state that he cannot see the world except as gravitating around him, at his service. We would be greatly mistaken if we viewed this universal phenomenon simply as a moral lack analogous to conscious (and no longer ingenuous and spontaneous) egoism; for it constitutes only a basic disposition of a being which is beginning to emerge from its cocoon but is not yet open to social life.

In opposition to egoism, egocentrism in no way

excludes generosity. The egocentric child *does not think* of being generous, because he is not yet turned naturally toward others. But a teacher merely has to open the child's eyes to the human world and the child's natural generosity will be manifested in a very lively fashion.

Contrariwise, the egoistical child and adolescent (or adult) *will deliberately refuse* any generous act we might suggest to them, even when they might be aware of being able to do something well. The egocentric does not think of going out of himself; the egoist refuses to do so.

This egocentric attitude is at the basis of numerous manifestations which seem strange to us in the child's mental life. We will return to this in the second part of our study. What we must realize now—and we cannot insist too much on it—is that *egocentrism is a normal attitude for every child under seven or eight years of age,* and that this attitude does not present any danger, at least if it does not persist a good deal beyond the age of nine or ten.

But to take this factor into account does not mean giving in to all the child's caprices, sitting by while he becomes a tyrant in the home, and *transforming this egocentrism into a perduring egoism* by excessive over-indulgence. Often it is the blundering of educators, parents or teachers, and very frequently their culpable indulgences, which catapult the child into true egoism.

In modern family education too much attention and indulgence is lavished on the child. He must be made to understand that there are other people on earth besides himself who merit attention. Beware of the only child! It is not always easy to make him see others as worthy of attention, concern, effort, sympathy or gifts. Accustomed as he has always been to be the object of the efforts of all those around him, he is more prone than other children to a profound egoism and to jealousy.

This is even more the case when the mother of an only child generally accepts her son's normal and desirable progressive emancipation with much more difficulty than the mother of a large family. The same is true of a chronically sick child who is accustomed to more assiduous care than that given to his brothers and sisters, and who does not often have the chance to see other people.

The teacher's task is thus to facilitate the passage from egocentrism to altruism on the social plane and the passage from the subjective to the objective viewpoint on the intellectual plane. The teacher will foster this normal evolution by permitting the child to have a good many contacts with other children of all ages as well as with nature, plants and animals.

The child must be helped to discover these relations between things and people which he does not yet know. And this does not take place without some lumps! A baby will not understand that fire burns until he has burnt himself; in like manner must the child—in order to discover the social attitude which he should take—come up against his companions and adults; he must discover for himself the will of another, his needs, his miseries, his cruelty or his goodness.

We must foster this discovery of the material and human world which will gradually draw the child out of himself. This regression of egocentrism is natural; however, care must be taken to facilitate it, for the actual surroundings do not encourage it.

4. *The child lives in the present.*

This is entirely natural: his past is still too limited

for him to be able to think about it. As for his future, he cannot get a really accurate idea of it until he has constructed the present which is all about him—of which the future will be only a prolongation. The child's whole being is in the state of perpetual becoming, in continual tension toward something better. But there is no implication that he is conscious of this and that his thought is directed toward a future which until the age of thirteen or fourteen holds little interest for him.

Such are the facts taught us by current experience. But if we observe the child's behavior as closely as possible, we will discover that this "life in the present" is really a stage in the life of the individual, a stage corresponding to a stage of psychical maturation completely different, for example, from the stage of the adult who lives in the future.

The passage from the habitual orientations of the spirit from the present to the past and then to the future characterizes the major stages of ascending life (from birth to adulthood); just as the reverse passage from the future to the past and then to the present characterizes the stages of declining life (old age).

We will see then that the broad outlines of child psychology which we have sketched in this "static part" are in reality only the most visible dominants of a continuous evolution which we will now study in detail.

The Fine Art of Teaching

Even when school has succeeded in inculcating only the bases of all intellectual effort (reading, writing, simple arithmetic); even when it has run aground in its efforts to teach good spelling usage, or has not been able to have the date of the Boston Tea Party or the battle of Bunker Hill committed to memory, it will already have achieved a fine work by cultivating in the child the ardent curiosity which is natural to him.

Textbooks, dictated notes, and synthetic expositions dull curiosity and enthusiasm. A few minutes a day will suffice for a mother to answer the questions of her children. She will then retain a great influence over them and they will not be tempted to seek elsewhere for answers to their legitimate curiosity.

Those who are instructors should realize that your troop is not a battalion. You will enrich your children much more if each day you give them something new to discover in which their personal curiosity will be satisfied on contact with the real. Real life is no more in a marble courtyard than it is in the thick of a desert wood.

As for those who are catechists, are you convinced that your children are curious about all these things of God and eager to find responses to their moral problems? Then do not suffocate them with your formulas, your morals or your theology. Lead them in the way, teach them about Life.

PART TWO

THE STAGES
OF THE CHILD'S
DEVELOPMENT

INTRODUCTION

1. The child is a being in constant evolution. We should not consider him as fixed or stable: if this year he has lost his enthusiasm, some other year he will express the contrary. Therefore, we should not be overly deceived by the ups and downs, the inevitable changes, in the mentality of each child.

2. In a study which seeks to sketch chiefly the psychology of the school ages of eight to fifteen, it might seem ridiculous to deal with the child from his first few years, or months. However, we must realize that *it is impossible to have a good understanding of the child if we do not know the psychology of his first few years.*

The age that concerns us is only one link in a chain, a compromise between two states, a period which still reverberates with the results of shocks experienced during the previous periods. Some have affirmed that the child of seven has acquired virtually all the character traits of his future personality.

Certainly, the child still remains perfectible, and happily so. However, we will see that numerous moral qualities and numerous intellectual attitudes will be lost if they have not been acquired before this age. If his education has been inadequate before the age of seven, it then becomes increasingly more difficult to recover the time lost and to walk the path again out of its due time. Before the age of six or seven, the child's education can already be either solidly established or almost irreparably compromised.

3. The general pace of the child's growth does not constitute a straight and regular line. It includes rapid or slow curves, levels, crises and jolts. We will distinguish principally the periods of regular growth and the crises, which will be for us the easily recognized landmarks of an evolution depicted in its basic aspects.

We can represent this evolution broadly by a graph (see p. 148), but we must at no cost attribute a mathematical value to it. The periods of acquisitions in particular are subject to considerable advance or retardation. Although they are represented only by a point on the curve, they sometimes last a long time.

A graphic presentation has at least the advantage of clearly demonstrating the following.

A. During the almost regular periods of growth (represented by the oblique lines), the development is less and less rapid and becomes slower with age, finally ceasing after the age of fifteen for those who stop all intellectual effort at this age. This development continues till the age of seventeen for the functions of automatism, and till the age of twenty-five for the functions of abstract thought on condition, however, that such faculties are continually exercised.

B. Crises (represented by the degrees) are

more and more violent till the age of eighteen and progressively more lengthy.

C. During these crises one cannot judge a growth or setback. The characteristic instability of these periods sometimes exhibits a sudden and brusk development in some specific aspect of personality and sometimes, simultaneously, a temporary setback in some other.

4. *These crises are symmetrical.* They recur in an analogous fashion and involve with more or less gravity the same dangers and the same consequences.

If the adult is struck by these crises, it is because they are *above all* in *the social order,* that is, in the child's relations with those about him, in his discovery of the human world. Other crises exist in the psychology of the child—particularly, in his intellectual or moral development; but the adult does not notice them so much because they are less externalized and do not always create an opposition between the child and himself. We will see that the intellectual crisis generally comes a little before the social crisis, and is followed by the moral crisis.

Finally, we must note that one of the frequent consequences of these crises is the appearance of emotional conflicts. The most common and the easiest to discern is the group of psychological manifestations described by the name "inferiority complex." With reference to each crisis, we will see how it can appear and the remedies that can be used against it.

We should realize in advance, however, that if these complexes are not "liquidated" before the subsequent crisis, they are aggravated by the latter and become more and more difficult to uproot; they can then scar a child for life.

The Fine Art of Teaching

Have confidence in this child who is not yet weighed down by the mediocrity and egoism of the adult world. Have confidence in these new powers which germinate in the young being like the seed of future harvests. Have confidence in all that can slake this intense thirst for progress: passion for games, curiosity, imagination, love of fighting, etc.

Is evil present? Original sin, bad example, greatly weakened will and difficulty of perseverence? Of course. And let us not forget it! But why should we also forget grace? Children are filled with God's gifts. Their whole being is directed, consciously or not, toward growth and all that is best. Why should we ignore their attraction toward the beautiful and the good? Why this pedagogy of pessimism?

Have confidence in the child! Have confidence in the enormous power for progress on the part of a new being filled with passions and desires. Have confidence in a being captivated by the beautiful and excited by the good. Have confidence in him whom life has not yet "wised up," bored, discouraged, beaten, deadened and confirmed in mediocrity.

And what of the others? Have confidence in them too—the dull, bored, timid, discouraged, fearful and sad. Have confidence in them despite everything! Believe in them; this is not to become blind. The atmosphere which we establish around them—this climate of joyous energy—will impart to them the enthusiasm and interest for the effort, joy and purity which they will lose in an unhealthy environment.

Have confidence, hope patiently for the bud to blossom, see in this child all the good of which he is capable, and provide him with the occasion to affirm these emerging qualities. Education is a Faith.

Hence, to achieve this confidence is to show oneself worthy of that honor which is the consideration or admiration of a child. This can be done only at the price of a constant effort toward true holiness. The progress of the child is achieved only through the progress of the teacher. To have the child rise toward the best means to ascend before him and lead him in one's wake.

FROM BIRTH TO
THE AGE OF THREE

Birth is an enormous shock, followed by a considerable effort at physical adaptation: respiration and the pulmonary circulation of blood must be established in minutes before the orifice between the two auricles closes. In a few days, the digestive organs must absorb their first meals.

This shock—even in seemingly healthy infants—may be the source of future mental anomalies: convulsions, dizziness, momentary unconsciousness and especially epilepsy which may appear several years later (in the case of epilepsy, between fourteen and eighteen) and which are often the result of the traumas of birth.

The child does not enter life with all his faculties perfected and simply slumbering. He arrives with "factors of orientation" which by the vital force of his being normally and gradually create functions that are still inexistent: birth is only a stage in a continuous evolution from conception to adulthood. This is true of the physical as well as the psychical aspect.

The initial age is the age of first discoveries. *Discovery of motion* first of all: the infant squirms and moves his members with evident pleasure. This exercise is necessary for his whole muscular, neuro-motor or mental development. Hence, babies are no longer left in tight swaddling clothes the whole day long.

The discovery of his own motion and all that stirs leads to the *discovery of his body*. The infant sucks, touches, handles, squeezes. He looks at his moving hands (four months), and one day he succeeds in touching his feet (about six months).

He discovers the *immediate space around him:* first of all, he hears sounds and sees light (first weeks), then begins to let his eyes follow luminous objects, things in motion, and turns his head toward sounds. Between three and seven months he is fascinated with the contours of the crib, the bars on his bed, the ruffles of the mosquito net. He touches, handles, sucks all these things for hands, eyes and mouth are associated in this exploration.

Gradually, he discovers *three-dimensional space:* he progressively draws out the picture of the world which he presses to his body. What infant has not stretched out his arms to grab the lamp, the tree in the garden or the moon? Thanks to his actions, his first movements (on all fours at nine months, he walks by himself without help around the thirteenth month), he constructs the third dimension, depth.

At the same age the infant *discovers the word*. He becomes aware all at once of curious sounds that his mouth can produce, and so begins the "lingual game" which tirelessly repeats the same sounds and syllables. Even if "ma-ma-ma" rises often to his lips, this has no meaning before ten or twelve months. He is incapable of handling the symbolism of words, of understanding that words represent objects.

The first words will gain a content, an intention, around the age of twelve months; he will begin to connect them two by two around the age of two.

The small child is endowed with *considerable emotionality*. Everything causes a shock to him: noise, newness, anything sudden, cessation of some usual thing, change in the regimen (weaning). According to their bruskness and their repetition, these shocks can leave their traces on his character: retarded mental and physical development, abnormal nervousness and instability, insecurity complex, fears, timidity, phobias. We still see the consequences today of the bombardments of the last war which have shaken the nervous systems of those who were infants at the time.

It is important to insist on the appearance at this age of the *sentiment of order and disorder*. Among the shocks which we have just mentioned, those stemming from disorder, instability and irregular hours, are the most frequent and are experienced by the child as a form of insecurity and anguish. Placed as they are in the vast chaos of the surrounding world that is incomprehensible to them, these little ones have no other "points of reference," no other stable aids than those of regular habits, of things found in their place, of actions done in the same order, of prohibitions which allow of no exceptions.

It is a shock for the infant suddenly to see his mother wearing a hat when he has always seen her bareheaded. It is a shock of the same order as finding his bed in an unfamiliar room or sleeping in a new crib. Useless changes should be avoided, and the infant must be helped to surmount necessary ones by reassuring him (need for security).

Toward three years of age, the child plays at disarranging and rearranging piles of linen, blocks and alignments of buttons. It is at this age that he finally discovers that order is something which is established or undone at will. But it is much earlier than the age or three, from the first few months, that the child must be placed in a framework of life as regular as possible. The child who has lived this period in disorder, without real schedule, and with an irregular sleeping routine, his difficulty in adapting to these continual changes. Disorder disturbs and upsets; order appeases and calms.

This regular training which we are urging prepares from the earliest weeks and enormously facilitates *obedience* in the future. If something is one day allowed by the adult and the next prohibited, first tolerated and then punished, the child is profoundly shocked and will inevitably acquire a difficult, nervous, disobedient and contentious character.

In summary, this first age is the time when the infant acquires indispensable automatisms. His life is a tissue of habits, formulated very precociously, which form the basis for his knowledge of the world around him and his first relations with adults. He still remains isolated, but knows when necessary how to provoke the reactions of the adult by a certain number of practical attitudes, cries, tears, caprices, smiles, and by a few common words or other less poetical manifestations.

We can therefore realize that through the routine of these procedures of summary exchanges, and the stability of his life habits, this age effects a great part of his development and his future equilibrium.

THE CRISIS OF
THE AGE OF THREE

First steps toward autonomy

Until the age of three, the child has been gradually discovering and constructing the space around him. Thus, he finds himself capable of an initial degree of autonomy: he scurries all around, tugs at the table-cloth covered with dishes, and breaks his first glasses. This is the age when parents prudently barricade the stairs, or clear away all fragile objects which have not yet been safely tucked away, and when they are continuously shouting at the top of their lungs: "Don't run; you'll fall!"—"Don't touch that, you'll get all dirty!" —"Watch out, you'll get hurt!"

Tell me, now, what would your head feel like if someone were to yell these things over and over at you, for example, the week after a long illness when the doctor had allowed you to take a few steps in your room? You would do just what the child does, and this would increase your desire to move around, investigate everywhere, touch everything. Only, in your case it would not be called a caprice and you would not be spanked. But you would be inclined—like the child— to go beyond what the doctor had allowed.

The three-year-old masters the space of his daily life and abruptly experiences the altogether natural desire to profit from it. This results in an avalanche of commands, warnings, threats or punishments which the parents believe necessary. And very naturally the child, bullied by his needs for "spatial expansion" and shut up in an empty room, has only one desire—to break these barriers and break something else too.

We have insisted above on the absolute necessity of functional exercise for the child's development. The three-year-old seeks to discover the world and he is prevented from doing so! I am courting disaster if I say that the child of this age needs to run everywhere, touch everything, break anything that can be broken, and use his crayons on something. But it is true! Then, for goodness sake, let him *garner his experience;* only, do not place him in a Louis XV salon in the midst of porcelains by Saxe!

It is therefore between two-and-a-half and four years of age that the child—gradually disassociating himself from the world around him and from his family —clears the first stage toward autonomy. This is the initial phase of the discovery of objectivity.

This also constitutes the *first crisis of opposition:* a person cannot achieve even partial autonomy without opposing those who previously gave him their protection. And it is normal; this crisis of opposition is correspondingly more violent and more marked by caprices to the extent that the parents continue to keep the child in a situation that can no longer be his because it is too confining for his need of activity.

The crisis of the age of three is the first serious conflict between the child who feels the need to free himself a little and the parents who feel the need to look more seriously upon his pranks which are now dangerous for tableware. There is "dogged opposition" between the parties facing one another.

Does this mean that the child must be left free to break what he pleases, to mark the doors with sticky and blackish imprints, and to draw on walls? I would not dare to say as much. It is essential for this child's development that he be able to exercise all his senses and muscles which develop very quickly at this age. Hence, put him in a yard or someplace where there is no risk involved, which does not mean someplace that is empty!

On the contrary, place several objects there that can be manipulated in different ways: pebbles, sticks, nuts, marbles, pearls, strings, blocks, old magazines; let him in this way easily encounter the greatest number of varied experiences, and allow him for the most part the turbulence—free from danger—which is necessary for his development. It is the very great task of nursery schools and kindergartens to foster this development by abundant materials, while appeasing family conflicts.

Between forceful repression of caprices and unrestrained license, parents exhibit an entire gamut of attitudes toward the child of this age. But it is ironic to discover that the two extreme procedures lead pretty much to the same result and throw the child out of balance. If the adult intervenes for the slightest trifle and bears down with all the weight of his authority to crush the slightest caprice, either the child shrivels up and suffocates (source of deep mental anomalies), or —if the child is vigorous—the caprices multiply and the reactions of opposition become violent. This attitude on the part of the adult is therefore not the right one.

If, on the other hand, the adult pretends to be unaware of everything, overlooks all pranks, and lets the child eat and sleep as he wishes, we see a recrudescence of caprices. Everything occurs as if the child wished to "try" his parents, wanted to see "how far he could go." The fact that he encounters no obstacle seems to create a deep lack of satisfaction in the capricious child. With one stroke he upsets the whole established order whose indispensable stability we have mentioned on the preceding pages.

Thus, the child finds himself lost in chaos once again, his habits destroyed, his traditional props gone. The child whose caprices are all overlooked is vexed, sad, fretful, lost. He seems in a great deal of his conduct to regress to a previous stage; he remains a baby. The method of letting him do as he wishes is therefore not the best, either.

Between these two extremes there is still the method of "sometimes yes, sometimes no," that is, the absence of method. The mother shrieks and threatens to no avail for the child knows that she does not often keep her promises of punishment. She calls something disobedience one day but smilingly allows it the next day.

How can the child be expected to adjust to this? This is the method followed by many mothers! The child is placed in the impossible situation of fashioning a moral theology for himself, since a great many things are one day allowed and the next forbidden. He thus multiplies his caprices in the hope of making his mother give in through weariness. Such a child is then called "an impossible brat." But whose fault is that?

There remains the right method. It entails first of all giving the child a small set of intangible rules (going to bed when his mother says so, remaining quietly on his chamber pot, allowing himself to be washed without a fuss, refraining from entering certain places without permission, etc); secondly, keeping an eye on the child so that he will not run into danger (he is not yet sufficiently rational and experienced); but, thirdly, letting him do for the most part all the experimenting he wants except for the two restrictions mentioned above.

In cases of danger or grave wrongdoing, or further before an infraction of one of the "sacred rules" he has promised to keep (sleep, eating, etc.), a calm reprimand in an even but *inflexible* tone is more than enough.

In this way, authority never gives in. It is no longer tempted by the ease of "sometimes yes, sometimes no." Finally, it allows the child the possibility of the growth required by his age.

And there is never the need to promise candy. Nor should one fear loss of the child's affection by such an attitude. Certainly, the time for caresses should never be neglected. But the time of caprices is not such a time. And as for giving candy at every moment of the day, it will lead to stomach aches (and this is possibly the best way of making the child even more capricious).

Very often this first crisis of opposition against the child's environment is marked by various emotional troubles: hostility of the boy toward his father, accompanied by a more or less exclusive love for his mother and a more or less vague feeling of guilt (the reverse is true in the case of girls). This is what is commonly called the "Oedipus complex."

Such feelings will be so much the more marked to the extent that the father is harsher and more authoritative and the mother is weaker. A just balance must be maintained on the part of both between rigor and license. But the father must remain firm and the mother tender: the reversal of roles is an anomaly which does no good to the child's well-being.

At the same time, or a little later, the child manifests a feeling of jealousy toward his brothers and sisters which is sometimes striking (toys, place on his mother's lap, etc.). This jealousy, more or less mixed with feelings of inferiority, is often strengthened by the teasing or callousness of older children and by the abilities and easier achievements of a more gifted child.

More frequently than not, parents also intensify these conflicts by blundering reprimands or preferences for one or other child. This is even more true since these emotional difficulties often remain hidden and are interiorized by the child who has vaguely felt—rightly or wrongly—the guilt of these hostile impulses.

These abnormal manifestations are very frequent and should not surprise us; but they should disappear quickly. They are generally "liquidated," *compensated for,* by an increase of affection, by greater tenderness—but non-exempt from firmness toward caprices—and by discretion and the strictest equality in the distribution of caresses to brothers and sisters.[5]

Summing up, at the end of a period of elementary spatial discoveries the child finds himself in a position to acquire a certain autonomy. This leads to a first crisis of emancipation, around three or four years of age, marked by caprices which should not disturb us: *do not shout or cajole, but simply wait for it to pass.* During this period family conflicts often appear which will disappear before the age of five if the milieu does not harm the child's desire for autonomy.

---

[5] For example, it is beginning with the age of three or four the child must be gotten to admit without jealousy that not all members of the family are to be treated in the same way: six-year-old Peter will receive chocolate but not three-year-old Jeanie because it would not be good for her. A greater portion will be given to twelve-year-old Jimmy than to Peter. In short, beginning at this time the child should be taught *the sense of equity* rather than the sense of equality.

The Fine Art of Teaching

If you interrupt the child's effort at every moment to say: "Johnny, give me those matches," or "Johnny, don't make such a racket," do you not see that you stifle his energy and retard his abilities? It would be interesting to hear your reaction if the same things were said to you while you were stirring your sauce or reading your newspaper!

We should carefully refrain from interrupting the child every time a mosquito comes buzzing around. If he is occupied and not bored, what he is doing at the moment is more important for him than your work is for you. Respect what he does, encourage him, even if it seems useless to the rest of us. If we help him in his effort, he will gradually turn to more difficult tasks and—even if they should not be what we would have wished for him—they will enrich him if he puts his whole heart in them.

If his mind is working, and if his fingers, eyes or ears are busy, you must realize that nothing is useless for him that can give him a new idea or a new experience. Let him be —whether he is dissecting a tree leaf with his awkward fingers, or using a pebble on a hard rock, or following the chimney smoke with his eyes. This is the way he will learn things that we know, or that we do not know and will never know. He is building the Universe!

And our role is never to arrest this effort and perseverence, but always to encourage and channel it.

The Fine Art of Teaching

If you believe you are doing the right thing—because it is wise—in taking away from him everything that the child risks smashing, soiling or swallowing, he will always find something which you have failed to get out of the way. But if when he is five you give him the job of setting the table one day a week, he will break nothing (at least, no more than you usually do). Furthermore, he will have learned to maneuver without damage in the midst of these dangers by putting all of himself into the job. And he will have grown accordingly.

Pockets are a great invention. Let the child fill them with odd objects: through assorted pebbles he gradually discovers the notion of numbers and through a length of string the notion of measurement, much better than through us deformed adults who seek to stuff him with calculus or the metric system. Let him measure with feet, pebbles and strings before stupefying him with pounds and yards! Why do you exhaust your patience and the child's still considerable amount of goodwill with letters, numbers and hours which he cannot assimilate!

Wait until he is six years old before trying to teach him to read. Wait until he is seven or eight before showing him how to tell time. Otherwise, you will waste your time, weary his mind which is still not curious about such things, and make him disgusted with putting forth any effort.

SECOND CHILDHOOD FROM FOUR TO SEVEN

The years from four to seven constitute the second stable period of childhood and are those in which the child widens the sphere of his knowledge. In the preceding years he lived in chaos; gradually, the "things that interested him" emerged and he learned to conduct himself according to imposed attitudes, according to an ensemble of conditioned reflexes or immediate procedures.

The period from four to seven years of age is the one in which this chaos becomes organized by a real effort at understanding. Through contact with the spatial world which he has now mastered, the child continually enriches his mind and constructs the mental functions connected with memory.

Optimum age for sensorial receptivity

Until now the child had undergone the slow learning process of his body and its sensorial-motor functions. Henceforth, he will use them to the maximum extent. The data of the senses become more numerous if one has taken the trouble to provide him with the means to manipulate and observe something else besides the bare walls of a gloomy room.

The child of this age manifests a veritable avidity for the world; he notices countless details which the adult had never noticed; he plays at seeing, at hearing; he plays at touching, at breaking, at rubbing.

But in all this he has no system, and it is useless to give him one. The only law that counts for him is the fleeting curiosity of the moment; without continuity in his interests, he follows his fantasy of a butterfly.

There is nothing disquieting about this until the child is around five years old; at that time he begins to stay at the same task for longer periods if it conforms to his concrete interests of the moment. At this age, too, he always has great need for movement and play, since his mental development is linked with his motor activity at the same time that he manifests a great need for discoveries in his surroundings.

Formulation of new mental functions

During the child's first two years of life, his mental activity was reducible to the establishment of conditioned reflexes, analogous to Pavlov's dog (who manufactured saliva at the striking of the clock because he was conditioned to receive his food at this sound). During the period from three to seven years of age a new series of mental functions is organized. The data of the senses no longer have the sole effect of prompting reflexes connected with vegetative life; the perceptions become associated in the unconscious, arrange themselves according to laws which are still not very well known to us, and are henceforth utilized no longer on the plane of automatisms, but also on *the plane of memory*.

The sensorial data are now ordered—not according to a logical plan but by random encounters and relations. This unconscious structurization based on external contributions produces the rich imagination of the five- to eight-year-old child (until the school kills this imagination by stamping out his curiosity and fantasy).

One of the most striking characteristics of this age is a *love for dreams and fairy tales*. We should provide healthy and abundant fare in this sphere which will later allow originality in creative thought.

The danger of excess remains tied in not with intellectual troubles but with emotional troubles which must be taken care of: the child deprived of affection, hurt and isolated, withdraws into his dreams which he finds more to his liking than his real surroundings. Gradually, he fails to adapt himself to life and isolates himself: the remedy—like the cause—must come from the emotional order.

A frequently misunderstood manifestation of this vivid imagination is the apparent prevarication of many children in this age-group. The following example is typical:

A six-year-old sets out with his father for a walk in the park. On leaving, he tells his mother: "We're going to see the swans!" Indeed, the swans in the pond are his favorite reason for walking in the park. But when they get to the park at the edge of the pond, there are no swans! They have gone back into their shelter because of the cold. The child and his father walk around the pond, but the swans do not make an appearance. So they return home, and the first thing the child says to his mother is: "Mommy, we saw the swans!"

What is the conclusion of all this? The child has taken his desire for reality. If his father points out his error to him, the child persists in saying the same thing but ultimately gives in with sorrow. *Here there is no question of a lie* in the meaning we give to this word which is charged with moral reprobation.

Even though the child's desire may not always be so apparent, it very often happens that he pursues his thought and embroiders reality: the dog he saw was blue and everyone ran out of fear; the lady had a long feather like this on her hat, etc. The child follows the suggestions of his imagination and desires, just as without giving it a thought he sometimes follows the suggestions of his environment and the persons he listens to.

The fault does not lie with his moral sense which has not yet been developed, but with his imagination which is *not yet controlled, overwhelmed, by the critical sense*. The thought of this age is bereft of objectivity, for two reasons: (1) first of all, because the child does not make a clear distinction between true and false; (2) secondly, because he is extremely subjective, that is, because he imparts to everything the color of his desires in accord with his whim of the moment.

The remedy for this kind of truth-twisting is never found in punishment but in the attitude of the adult who helps the child always to follow his statements with a judgment such as: "It's true" or "It's not true," and aids him to determine the veracity of his statements by the facts themselves. But it is a work that will have no lasting effects before the age of eight or nine.

In any case, three principal kinds of lies must be distinguished: lies caused by one's imagination, lies for one's safety (prompted by the fear of punishment by adults), and lies intended to deceive. These constitute three degrees of gravity that require three very different remedies.

It is always true that the materials ceaselessly

streaming through the sense organs are composed, arranged, regrouped and associated, ready to be utilized at a more or less distant date by the memory which will recall them in order, or by the imagination which will assemble them in another manner. The end of this period will usher in the *age of the "why"* in which the child of six or seven continually pesters those about him *a propos* of everything and nothing.

Very often he hardly listens for the reply (all the more since this is frequently furnished him by dint of inaccessible logic and abstract explanations). It is no less necessary for adults to take the trouble to answer him, and to answer in terms that he can understand.

A mother need only send her son away with a "You're boring me to death!" to cause him to lose all curiosity little by little and ultimately all confidence. When other more troublesome questions arise to assail the child, he will seek their answers in dictionaries or elsewhere.

Egocentrism

The period between four and seven represents the splendid age of egocentrism, that ingenuous candor in egoism which we have mentioned in the first part of this study. It is not a question merely of an *emotional and social disposition* on the part of the child which turns everything to his service. It is a question above all of an *intellectual disposition* which considers everything, things and persons, in terms of oneself. Thus, when the child is about eight years old, the following conversation might take place:

1) "Do you have any brothers and sisters?"
   "Yes, a brother, Paul, and a sister, Jeanie."
2) "How many brothers and sisters does Paul have?"
   "He has a sister, Jeanie."

3) "He has a brother, too, doesn't he?"
"No."
4) "How many brothers does Jeanie have?"
"One brother: Paul."

This test shows that the child does not count himself, for he does not disassociate himself from the world about him. On the day—around the age of eight or nine—when he answers correctly, his egocentrism will have a good chance of having become a conscious egoism. He will no longer be at the center of the world; he will refer the world back to himself. At least—let us hope—if the family circle has allowed the child's normal evolution toward objectivity and altruism. Egocentrism should thus disappear between the ages of eight and twelve, at the price of remaining with the adolescent and the adult in the wake of egoism.[6]

There is another very precocious manifestation of egocentrism. Around the age of three the sharp sense of ownership appears: toys, clothes, spoon, plate, etc. Furthermore, with the arrival of a little brother or sister the child exclaims, "She's *my* Mommy," with a conviction which makes it clear that she is not the Mommy of "the other one." This instinct for ownership is also a compensation for his inferiority complex in relation to his brothers and sisters: his personality is built up, augmented, by all that belongs to him. To possess something means in his eyes to grow so much bigger.

We must not combat this affirmation of ownership too quickly (not before the child is six years old), at the risk of obtaining the contrary effect and rooting a deep sense of dissatisfaction in the child's mentality.

---

[6] We should note that this *unconscious* egocentrism will frequently reappear much later in the grave crises which require the mobilization of all the forces of one's being, as in major illnesses, in danger or in the realm of fear.

The age of the "why" marks the still confused emergence in the child of a notion of causality which he will not master before nine years of age. For the moment everything remains quite illogical and very much tied in with momentary mobile emotions; above all, it is very much connected with *magical beliefs* which means that in the mind of the five- or six-year-old to speak or think of anything involves really acting on that thing itself.

The egocentrism which we have just mentioned lies at the basis of an entire intellectual phenomenon that pervades the child's whole mentality. It is at the origin of numerous manifestations that seem bizarre to us adults, such as *animism*.

Until about the age of five, the child regards as living and conscious all the things around him (sun, pebbles, water; animals, houses, etc., without distinction); until the age of six or so, he persists in the belief that all moving bodies are conscious (bicycle, smoke, etc.). These beliefs will slowly and progressively disappear only around the age of seven or eight.

Another (almost simultaneous) consequence of egocentrism is *artificialism*. This is the belief whereby the child attributes to every being and every object an original maker in a human form. A very big and powerful man has dug the beds for rivers, pushes the sun forward, and blows the wind. Furthermore, it should be noted that this takes place even before the adult environment has inculcated in the child a belief in an all-powerful God.

Very often, the result of this superimposition of natural beliefs and adult teachings is a curious blend which formulates a theology for the child that is not always very orthodox: the good God, about whom adults speak, has fabricated all things with his hands, using the identical tools we do, and when necessary has gone to the store and bought the seeds for the plants which he causes to grow, etc. There is no reason to become alarmed by these naïvetés which will gradually be left behind.

It would take a long time to describe the countless forms of this infantile egocentrism. Besides magic, animism and artificialism, we can also note *finalism*. This refers to the fact that in the child's mind every object is "made for" a human usage, and has a role to play in our lives (definitions by usage: cf. p. 35).

As for the consequences of egocentrism on the child's logic, we will speak of them again later on. For the present it is sufficient to say that the child below the age of seven or eight is incapable of mentally envisaging two objects at once. Where we see an ensemble of facts related to one another, he sees *successively* (and not at all simultaneously) objects connected together by nothing more than a vague juxtaposition.

This accounts for the child's characteristic incapacity to handle judgments of relation (for example, the right and left of the one speaking to him) because of his inability to place himself in a viewpoint other than his own. This also accounts for the countless contradictions common to infantile narratives in which the child unconsciously amasses judgments that are incompatible in our eyes; he has no conception of the relations possible between these affirmations.

Construction of the notion of time

One of the child's most delicate acquisitions takes place between four and eight years of age: the acquisition of the notion of time. Related to the functions of memory and association, this notion is connected with that of causality. It is acquired only gradually, through the observation of more or less rapid series and successions.

We will deal with it later on, at the same time as the other acquisitions of the ninth year. The understanding of time, which also presupposes the acquisition of the ability to read, will not take place before eight or nine years of age.

Development of the means of communication

When necessary, the development of the means of social communication will be speeded up to the same extent that the crisis of the age of three or four has been passed without incident and social pressures are less harmful.

Learning a language takes place between three and five years of age. It is by seeking to place himself in relation with others that the child learns to think and to clarify his ideas. However, we must note that language around the age of five is still a gratuitous game: very often, it is a monologue; and the child frequently cares precious little about being heard or understood.

The principal stages in the oral exchanges between two children of the same age can be presented in this way: isolated monologues, parallel monologues, interfering monologues and dialogues on the same subject but without relation to each other; finally, around the age of six or seven, dialogues with reciprocally adapted replies. Naturally, these various procedures are often employed at the same time and some of them subsist in the child's language until the age of ten or so. But progress is continual in this progressive socialization of language and thought.

Learning to write takes place between five-and-a-half and seven years of age. This is a complementary function of communication which if inculcated correctly by juxtaposing the oral word, the written word and the object will help the teacher to combat verbalism. This habit of the child to use at random words whose meaning he does not know is still inculcated by overly intellectual scholastic methods (absence of the concrete object) and by methods of teaching syllabic reading which, contrary to the global method, rivet the child's attention on the difficult letter rather than on the meaning.

Social development

Until the age of three, the child's social world is limited to the acquaintance of three or four people very close to him whom he loves in terms of the satisfaction to be found in them of his vital needs.

Although his world is enlarged a bit around the age of three or four and he becomes clearer and more precise in his thought, the child still has no social relations with other children: he scarcely likes to play *next to* other children of his age. But such relations are poor: consisting of imitation above all. His conversations are—when really listened to—more on the order of monologues. The child does not seek to make himself understood, expends very little effort to convey his thought and to inquire about that of others.

The social development is thus limited—and this is already considerable—to the acquisition of means of exchange or communication (word, drawing, writing, reading) which serve to manifest little more than his vital needs or curiosities. Hence, from the first stage of childhood to the second there is considerable progress from *autism* (isolation of an individuality who has not yet discovered the world about him) to *egocentrism* (the stage in which the child—having discovered his environment—still thinks it is uniquely made for him and does not bother about others). It is still a giant step to *altruism,* by which the child will desire to enter into the thought of others in order to understand them and, if possible, cooperate with them.

For the moment, the child's interest is centered entirely on the conquest of the material world, on a concrete acquaintance with the objects that surround him, on the progressive widening of his earthly horizons. This will constitute the great work of his mind until around the age of twelve. Later, he will turn his interests toward the human world.

From three to seven years of age the child discovers the material world with its individual isolated forces, and this is also a discovery of his personal possibilities and an awareness of the world through his body. From seven to twelve years of age he will be aided in this task by the collectivity of the children of his age. But only after twelve will his thought and interests become truly social and communitary.

Moral sense

Still only slightly developed, the child's moral sense is until the age of six connected chiefly with the remembrance of harsh reprimands and the fear of being spanked, rather than with a true sense of conscience. Until the age of six, the most important part of his education comes down to a kind of animal-training, to the acquisition of habits which will be so much the more rooted in the child insofar as they appear normal and natural to him. But for this to happen, it is still necessary that contrary examples not be too frequent (parents, older brothers and sisters, neighboring children), and that these habits be as stable as possible, allowing no exceptions (cf. p. 49).

Nevertheless, beginning with the age of five, it is possible to appeal to the child's affections and ask him to expend an effort "to make Mommy happy." Such a possibility should be cultivated very early and rely progressively on this affection to make the child realize his faults.

However, it could be dangerous to abuse this process if one fell into a kind of emotional blackmail which could cause the child to believe that a grave fault automatically provokes a diminution of his mother's love: "Oh, you're giving me such pain! ... Go to bed; I don't love you anymore!"

The child always needs love, even and especially to regain his courage after a mistake. It would be disastrous for his well being if he one day thought that he could no longer count on this affectionate and at the same time energetic help.

In any case, it is thoroughly useless to accompany commands and defenses with lengthy logical explanations. We have seen that this does not influence the child. The appeal to love for his mother is, on the contrary, much more accessible on condition that its efficacy is not abused by overly frequent use or for utterly futile reasons.

It seems also indispensable that the punishment never extend into the next day and that it be meted out without rancor or passion on the teacher's part. Punishment is sometimes necessary, but it must never be a subjective reaction of anger or irritation; it is a remedy that the teacher must apply dispassionately, just as the doctor administers his drug, objectively, for the sole good of the child.

Moral education at this age will only be effective if it requires merely a few points but requires them inexorably. In addition, it will only be real and lasting if it always stems from the strictest equity toward all the children; this sharp sense of justice appears around the age of five or six and will profoundly characterize the moral sense of the age that follows. It is one of the most solid "trump cards" of education.

The most important fact to note is that the moral sense of the seven- or eight-year-old is clearly different from our own:

● For the child, *guilt is attached to the act and not to the intention.* He does not understand that he is punished for wanting to pilfer a jar of preserves if he was not able to carry out his wish because of some fortuitous circumstance (for example, a chair that was too low to reach the shelf in the cupboard). The child is incapable of understanding that the intention of someone who commits a fault can enter into the appraisal of this fault. He develops in an environment that is too concrete for him to be concerned about intentions.

● *Culpability is attached to the act, no matter what its circumstances might be.* He does not really understand why he is forbidden to make noise in the room where his mother lies sick, when he was allowed to do so formerly and is also allowed to do so in other places.

● Consequently, the only punishment that counts is *an external, sensible, automatic and unavoidable and immediate punishment.* Before eight or nine years of age, the child does not appreciate the postponement of his punishment (he judges this to be a weakness). The mother's pardon must come after the punishment, not without it. The child does not understand, from the moment that he has perceived his fault, that the punishment will not be immediate.

It is only with the appearance of "secondariety"

71

and inhibition[7] (around the age of nine or ten or later) that the child will deeply feel the anxious waiting for a deferred punishment. This waiting could then be used —only in very grave and exceptional cases—to help him reflect and regret his fault.

If there were need of summarizing in a few lines the characteristics of the age between four and seven, we would insist on the fact that this whole period is dominated by egocentrism. Far from seeing in this attitude a moral lack (which the ill-chosen term wrongly suggests), we must maintain that *egocentrism is progress.*

First of all, it is *intellectual progress* since the child passes at this age from the noncomprehension of the world as chaos to an initial mental mode of organization. The three-year-old recognizes in the world only what pleases and interests him; he guides his behavior only according to concrete schemas destined to lead immediately to this pleasure or interest. Henceforth, the egocentric child gradually organizes his knowledge and sets up structures and a system for understanding the world.

Assuredly, this system has—in the view of our adult logic—the defect of being organized *around the*

---

[7] *"Secondariety"*: Possibility of reacting to a shock not immediately but later after a certain amount of delay; for example, "suppressed" wrath exploding after a delay, long grudges.

Inhibition: Voluntary power to check or stop intimate impulses. It is a negative will which renders the child capable of saying no to a temptation, suggestion or desire. The positive will (to do something) appears in the child sooner than inhibition (not to do something).

However, we must note that *reflective inhibition* often appears earlier: this is a sympton of emotional conflict and a dangerous manifestation for mental equilibrium. It is in this latter sense that we employ the term *inhibition* on pages 76-107 in regard to the feelings of inferiority during the periods of crisis.

subject, in relation to himself, in terms of himself, his interests and his experiences. But does this not represent enormous progress over the total absence of logic and comprehension? Certainly, this procedure is imperfect, and it calls for further progress which will take place during the age that follows; but at least it is a start toward understanding the world—a start which has been characterized as a *state of prelogic*— and it is better than the previous chaos.

Egocentrism thus represents *considerable social progress.* From the nonsocial state of the age below three the child passes to a *presocial state* which will continue until around the age of ten. He discovers persons, loves to approach other children, and practices the first exchanges of words or mutual aid. But these exchanges are isolated and are still a long way from achieving stable cooperation.

The child is interested in persons especially insofar as they can impede or foster his own enterprises. He organizes the social world and his social attitudes around his own interests, as he does the material world. Naturally, this is not the ideal charitable under-standing. But it is a great progress over the isolation of the first few months or the vague associations of the first few years between persons and the pleasure (or displeasure) which they can occasion.

The Fine Art of Teaching

At home, each child should have his little corner or at least his table and his own locked drawer which no one but himself can dig through. If he has no place in which to hide his findings and secrets, he will carry them in his heart, and his heart will be locked to you. Much better that it be a drawer!

We should regard the child as being at the halfway point, like a baby chick lost before having left its mother hen and the young stag who has escaped from the menagerie. We should take care above all to see that life fashions a rule of conduct for him which will not be the fruit of our injunctions, but of his own experiences. We should prudently economize the great influential power that we have over him. Whenever life can undertake without us to give him a useful lesson, we should allow life to do so!

Frankly speaking, we know very well that parental experience has been of such little value to us that we have been unable to censure him because of our own failures! Hence, we should save our power of persuasion for the areas in which life could warp this child: morals and religion. As for the rest, we should limit ourselves to protecting him from excessively dangerous experiences which would take the luster out of his eyes or leave him infirm.

The child, more than the adult, feels true goodness. In the face of the confused, suffering of this being who is too often harmed by those about him, we must not be content to provide a condescending thin-lipped smile now and then in the manner of one giving alms. We must frankly place ourselves in the child's heart and mind without backward adult thought, and speak right into his eyes the words that will put confidence back into his broken heart. His look and his smile will tell us if we have discovered how to deserve the honor of his confidence. For it *is* a great honor.

THE CRISIS
OF THE
AGE OF SEVEN

Second step toward autonomy

At the time of the preceding crisis, the child makes the discovery of what is usually called his "familial I." Between the ages of six and eight he makes the discovery of his "social I."

We will see that this crisis is not situated wholly *on the social plane,* but at least as much *on the intellectual and physiological planes.*

From the physical point of view, this age is a period of rapid growth. The child often exhibits a lean and scrawny aspect which is accompanied by a fairly high susceptivity to invasions of microbes. It is the age of otitis, appendicitis, and tuberculosis. This susceptivity is all the more regrettable inasmuch as the child is exposed to new and more numerous sources of contamination. Sicknesses incurred at school multiply, if they have not already been brought home by older brothers and sisters: measles, chicken-pox, mumps, flu, etc.

These breakdowns of health are a primary source of psychological difficulties, though very often only slight: irregular courses of study, creating difficulties of readaptation with each return to school and delays in finishing the courses; emotional instability of the child, plunged anew through sickness into conditions of dependence and "forced egocentrism"; missing stages in the learning processes or the normal interests of this age, especially as regards sociability.

These "missed stages" in the case of the child who has remained sick for a long time can be the cause of a real lack of adaptability to conditions of normal life. The ferocity of children and adults who have been gravely ill between six and ten years of age is characteristic. A missed stage is made up with difficulty, we have said, and can sometimes scar one's whole life.

As far as the *intellectual development* is concerned, the seven-year-old now masters the concrete world all about him. His corporeal activity and sensorial receptivity—both enormous during the preceding years—have caused him to discover his material environment. We will see the considerable acquisitions that this continual contact will henceforth allow.

From the intellectual point of view, the child now possesses the mental functions to navigate in space and time: especially, memory and imagination. He is on the way to conquering the world of ideas and this will be the great work of the following stage.

It also happens at this same age that the child enters school (at least around the age of six). There he discovers—sometimes a bit suddenly—that he is no longer the center of interest as in his family, but that he is just one among many others. This represents a real shock, going from his role as the center of attraction to that of a supernumerary, if not a walk-on!

Hence, coinciding with better established mental possibilities, the social universe opens up very abruptly for the child; and especially inasmuch as he no longer has the right, as he did at the age of five, to monologue and play alongside others like him but must now enter into real relations with them and adhere to an entirely new discipline.

Even for children who were prepared for these social contacts by their mother's schooling or by life in the street and thus did not experience such a rude shock, it is no less true that beginning school constitutes a very abrupt change of discipline and method, a passage without transition from the "family" style to the style of "school work."

In short, the great social progress of this period consists in passing from the confused relations of familial *dependence* (on the part of the child toward his parents), or of *superiority* between brothers and sisters of various ages to the much more delicate relations between *equals*. In this sense, we can say that the child passes through a *second phase in the discovery of object and subject,* in the disassociation of his personality and the world around him.

The crisis of the age of six or seven is thus a second stage on the way toward both the *mental autonomy of a spirit which henceforth masters the concrete* and its *social autonomy by the discovery of relations of equality.*

Hence, it constitutes the *second crisis of opposition:* one cannot affirm his autonomy without opposing those who have been caring for him. We purposely repeat the same terms we used to describe the crisis of the age of three. We could not insist too strongly on the symmetrical character of these troubled stages, since the same phenomena are reproduced with the same dangers and analogous remedies.

The period of the age of six or seven is also that of family conflicts, oppositions to brothers and sisters, caprices and jealousies, and above all difficulties of a boy with his father. Feelings of inferiority reappear and undergo a recrudescence corresponding in acuteness to the degree that beginning school constituted a shock, or that the parents were more intractable and less understanding.

This will often be expressed—before people and especially before the father (in the case of a boy)—by an attitude of inhibition characterized by *stammering,* jerky gestures, shifty and fearful looks, an attitude difficult to determine, an incoercible awkwardness, and *bad habits* which are more frequent and deep-rooted in proportion as the emotional conflict is more serious.[8]

Note that if these symptoms perdure for more than a year, it is because the complex does not disappear so quickly. It should disappear completely before the next crisis, before the age of twelve; otherwise, it will leave the child inhibited and in a state of inferiority *for life.*

We can counterbalance the feelings of inferiority that threaten and weaken the child and help overcome

---

[8] We might note in passing that stammering is almost always connected with left-handedness. It appears *in the left-handed child* at the precise age when on the one hand social difficulties arise to trouble the nice balance of the preceding age and when on the other hand scholastic disciplines wrongly force the child to use his right hand contrary to his innate dispositions of left-handedness. Stammering will manifest itself with much more gravity and persistence to the extent that the injunctions of parents and teachers are more violent in demanding that the child use his right hand. On the contrary, it is *indispensable* for the emotional and intellectual balance of this child that he use his preferred (left) hand for all current usages (eating and *writing*).

We can gather the frequency of such cases which have nothing exceptional about them, if we remember that six to eight per cent of all children are born with a left motor predisposition: that is, in a class of some thirty pupils, there are almost certainly two children who are taught to write with the wrong hand, and thus troubles of character are invited.

them by the same means used during the preceding crisis as well as by a few others. We must give the child a means of affirming his usefulness and superiority: an increase of affection without weakness, strict justice in dispensing a certain amount of overindulgence; nevertheless, we must show a very slight preference for one who, just as a sick person, has need of more sustained affection.

It is also by introducing the child into contact sports wherein his body will loosen up that we will draw out a boy of this age. And it is by rhythmic dancing, life in the open air, and giving her mother a hand that a girl who has retired into herself will open up once again.

At home, if the father yells: "You're good for nothing!" the best way to avoid a conflict or a withdrawal on the part of the child is to confer on him responsibilities in accord with his ability (setting the table, helping with the cleaning or with the dishes, etc.). He can then be proud of these chores, provided they are presented to him as an honor to serve the family cause and certainly not as drudgery.

Sometimes, the child himself will (unconsciously) choose his own compensations: he will thrash his younger brother as he himself has been thrashed by his father or grandfather (beaten and unfortunate children are not very tender toward others). Or he might take refuge in some hidden corner of the house or yard and there collect a little treasure of odd objects: string, pebbles, clothespins, gathered from heaven knows where and carefully hidden from the hostile gaze of anyone.

He may also take refuge in dreams and fiction (mythomania) or multiply "generous thefts" to provide gifts for his friends, to dazzle them and gain the admiration he seeks. Or, further, he may develop a taste to see animals suffer; he will torture his cat or pull his dog's tail. We must see to it that the child finds other less anti-social compensations.

We should add—something very important for the teacher—that this social crisis of the eighth year goes hand in hand with a *moral crisis* of more or less violent proportions. For a person does not sever his social relations with his family in such a harsh manner and accustom himself to those of school without a profound backlash of morality stemming from new obligations and the discovery of such particular and strict codes of the child group. Nevertheless, we must see in this crisis a more definite and precocious source within the family itself.

For, around the age of seven, the child has very suddenly made an initial painful discovery concerning his father whom he had previously regarded as well-nigh all-powerful, omniscient and eternal as well as concerning his mother who also bore the halo of incomparable perfection and goodness. He has per-ceived that his parents—who previously manifested in his eyes that ideal of supermen which every child carries within him and readily places at the origin of all creation—are not perfect at all, that they do not know everything and that they cannot do everything!

As unlikely as it might seem to our adult mental-ity, this produces a very great shock which is possibly more acute in children from environments in which education is taken seriously. The children then dis-cover with amazement, and even with real anguish and deep shock, the disputes of their parents. Pity those divided homes which almost infallibly provoke moral and emotional troubles in their children.[9]

---

[9] This discovery is much more precocious (after the age

81

This shock leads to the following very sad and all-too-frequent fact: children of this age group very often lose confidence in their parents and close up forever. From this stem the real lies and the first secrets: previously, the child concealed nothing, and did not even think anything could be concealed, since his parents knew everything (the myth of the small accusing finger).

In Christian family circles, this need to believe in an all-powerful superman is easily transferred to the idea of God-the-Father-Almighty and the Blessed Virgin Mary, both bearers of all the perfections which the child has been unable to attribute to those about him. The years from seven to ten are those of a very profound religious development which aids the moral stabilization of the child.

In this sense, at least, it is very useful that school and the discovery of new social relations provide the child of this age group with a powerful derivative and a source of new interests. It is still necessary that in this critical time of the child's life there be nothing too violently harmful which would scar his personality for a long time.

---

of five) where notorious conduct, alcoholism and disputes force the child to judge his parents. Thus children of divided homes are precociously awakened by these realities which are not made for them.

The Fine Art of Teaching

If you close your eyes when the child tells his first intentional lie, because you do not like to punish and out of pity for his weakness, tomorrow he will tell you whatever he wants in order to escape your reprimands. You will lose his confidence, because he will sense that you are weak and not really clairvoyant. In addition, he may also sense in some confused way that you have failed in your duty and rendered him a disservice.

Every ten-year-old has to some extent or other "swiped" a pen, eraser or pencil from one of his classmates. This does not necessarily mean he deserves a prison term. But to put an end to this habit, the best punishment is one which makes up for the harm caused: the surreptitious return of a better eraser purchased by him through his own economizing.

If such petty larcenies become more frequent, see a psychologist: this often indicates a need for emotional compensation.

Trust the child's sense of justice; it is sometimes sharper than your own. When the child is seven or eight, he should be aided to admit his fault. When he is around ten or eleven, we should calmly and sedately ask him what punishment he thinks he deserves. In many cases he will be a harsher judge of himself than we would. In any case, this will be the best way in which we can have him weigh the gravity of his actions and lead him to responsible freedom.

The longer you put off intervening to correct this emerging fault, the more powerless will your hand be in repressing his inclination. For it is before the age of twelve that a loyal and honest man is formed.

THIRD CHILDHOOD FROM EIGHT TO TWELVE

These four years constitute the third calm period of the child's life and are characterized by a general stability. From the physical point of view, the child puts on weight more quickly than he grows (in contrast to the periods of crisis when he grew without putting on weight proportionately).

From the social point of view, the difficulties of the crisis of the age of seven have abated and the social life enriches the child. As far as the intellectual life is concerned, the stable character of this period allows considerable progress which will be described below.

The periods of crisis, such as the one through which the child has just passed, are difficult periods, full of battles, oppositions, instability and anxiety. Although they enable the child to *free himself* from excessively stringent ties, to experience new needs and to discover new spheres, these periods do not offer a calmness which is sufficient to aid the true adaptation to these needs, and new horizons. The crisis enables us to take a step forward, indispensable for the regularity of the stage that follows.

But this happy period reorganizes the world in a new way, the child makes immense discoveries and forges the tools of thought and behavior proper to this age; in short, *stability allows adaptation* which would be impossible in a period of crisis.

The years from eight to twelve are dominated by an evolution of considerable importance: the almost complete *disappearance of egocentrism*.

At the same time that the regression of egocentrism permits the integration of the child in the world of his fellow-children on the social plane, it leads the child on the intellectual plane into the world of thought and basic abstract ideas. We can therefore well understand that the considerable enrichment of this period might at times be compromised and often hindered by family conflicts which we have already mentioned and by social pressures which, weighing on the child's personality, prevent him from getting out of himself and opening out to the world, and shut him up in his emotional complexes.

Development of the functions of abstract thought

The first childhood brought about the acquisition of vital automatisms and practical behaviors; the second effected the concrete functions of the intuitive life (memory, imagination); and the third childhood is the time when the child acquires—only after lengthy effort—the functions necessary for abstract thought. We will see what this involves for some of the most basic notions.

1. Relativity of qualities

Until the child was around seven, he regarded the qualities of a person or thing as *absolute*. Thus, *right and left* were not understood as relative to the person envisaged. Until the age of seven, the child who knows his right hand is incapable of understanding that the right hand of the person talking to him is not on the same side, absolutely speaking, as his own.

This was one of the principal difficulties in the acquisition of the notion of time. The child did not understand why "today May 15" was called "tomorrow" yesterday, and will be called "yesterday" tomorrow. The words "yesterday," "today" and "tomorrow" were taken as absolutes rather than as relative and variable with the passage of time.

Similarly, until about the age of twelve at a minimum, the child gets lost in the comparisons (relative qualities) of the Burt test:

"There are three little girls. The first is lighter than the second and darker than the third."

"Which one is the darkest of the three?"

Whenever he does not offer an answer at random, the child says it is the third!

We realize that this sense of the relative and the absolute is indispensable for logical reasoning, and hence that this logical reasoning is an impossible operation for the child under ten or twelve. About this time, the necessities of social relations oblige the child to express what he thinks and his language becomes much more coherent, his relations surer, the logic of his narratives firmer, and reasoning becomes possible because his intellectual life is organized and unified.

2. Notion of causality

To the extent that the child of the previous age

group judged all things in reference to himself, attributing to everything living or dead qualities which he discerned confusedly in himself, to the extent of this same egocentrism did the child apply to natural phenomena the most varied and fantastic explanations.

Mixed in with these explanations, as we have seen, without any kind of logical connection were *animistic* conceptions (every being is endowed with life and intentions), *magical* practices (according to whose rites one can act on things and invite them to modify their behavior), *artificialistic* origins (quasi-manual creation of things), and *universal* finalism (things created to fulfill a function for man).

Around seven or eight, the child begins to make a more or less judicious choice among these affirmations. If animism perdures, it is restricted to objects in motion (ships, projectiles) and this motion has less and less of an (artificialistic) human origin: material bodies owe their motion to an internal dynamism as well as to external causes: clouds move forward by their own will and by their inner power while also being pushed forward by the air which they force back!

We see then what contradictions and what "vicious circles" can still occur in the thought of a seven- or eight-year-old. Yet it is to this same child that we propound grammatical rules and catechism formulas filled with the most formal logical expressions!

Only in the neighborhood of nine or ten will the child apply normal mechanistic expressions to natural phenomena: the tree moves, not because it desires to more nor because it has its own power to do so, but because the wind shakes it. And the wind exists not because of the birds or the trees or the moon or some superman, but because of more normal reasons inspired roughly by adult scientific data.

Previous to this age the child did not assimilate the explanations offered by the adult. Either he rejected them from his thought as some restraining foreign body or he reworked them in a highly fantastic manner, with his own personal beliefs, without departing from the latter.

It is in this sense that we might look upon the child as an inspired poet. By not imposing on his thought the barrier of a strict logic, he creates very original *random* associations between a hundred other things devoid of interest for us. But the child has no awareness of being a poet and his inspiration lapses into platitudes whenever we make him aware of his discoveries and invite him to renew them.

As a result of these charming fantasies, it is also customary to attribute imaginative qualities to the child. This is well-founded if it refers to ability to place himself in the unreal and move at ease in it (without ever seeing the frontiers of reality and fantasy—before six or eight years of age).

But it is false to attribute a truly creative imagination to the child, one capable of original thought. The child does not create with the desire or awareness of creating. The majority of his discoveries are direct imitations of what he has seen in his friends. And he also makes random associations which occasionally do seem felicitous to us. But, in reality, the world of the child is extremely routine, imitative and traditional. True creative imagination will be one of the gifts of adolescence.

3. Powers of logic

Reasoning, which necessitates the acceptance of a viewpoint other than the subjective or egocentric one, is in the process of affirming itself once the child discovers causality and relativity. Between the ages of nine and ten the words "because," "since" and "so," which are used in reasoning, make their appearance in the child's language. It is interesting to keep an eye on this appearance because it is an important stage of intellectual development.

The ten-year-old generally succeeds in answering the following questions:

"If this animal has a long tail, it is a mule or a horse."

"If this animal has long ears, it is a mule or a donkey."

"Well, this animal has long ears and a long tail, what is it?"

Previously, he would have replied most often that the three cases are possible.

For a very long time the child misconstrued the meaning of our syllogisms and the *because's* used by adults to answer his questions. The word "because" often had a sense analogous to "and so," that is, a sense of juxtaposition, without any causal relation.

All his explanations of the world were impregnated with "participations," secret interresonances between (even distant) simultaneous events (the fish's movement and the sound of the river were connected by some interaction). Likewise, the logical explanations of adults were understood as bringing into play links of close juxtaposition because the child misconceived the possible relations of cause to effect.

4. Coordination of relations

In an ensemble of facts, the child sees only a juxtaposition; rarely before the age of seven does he see a succession, and never before nine does he see relations. If, for example, you tell a story and interrupt it just before the end to ask the child to provide an ending, he manifests himself incapable of offering a logical denouement. Generally, he takes an episode that struck him or invents some sudden turn of events without any relation with those which we would rightly expect as a conclusion.

Similarly, when we invite a six-year-old to describe the picture before him, he does so as follows: "There is a hat, and a table, and a lady, and this and this . . ." Around the age of eight or nine he makes initial progress and associates: "There is a lady with a hat. She is next to the table." But only when he is about ten or twelve does the child tie everything together in a coordinated package: "There is a lady who is seated at a table to put her hat back on by looking in the mirror which is above the table."

Very early, the child associates two juxtaposed facts when he has the habit of seeing them together. Around the age of seven he is capable of applying a simple relation to these two facts—succession or direct causality, for example. But it will be several more years before he can simultaneously coordinate these two facts with others in a more complex ensemble of multiple relations.

Moreover, he will do this in a manner that varies greatly with the intellectual development or the actual state of fatigue on the part of the subject and according to the difficulties of the problem raised.

Hence, the Burt test (see p. 87) poses a difficult logical problem: he must join three persons with the help of four terms: More, less, dark, blond. Since the child does not have a sufficient habit of juggling these concepts and mentally replacing "more blonde" by "less dark," for example, it is certain that this problem remains almost completely outside his grasp.

To take the example of a simpler problem, the child under eleven will not be able to affirm that if A = B and B = C, it is certain that A = C (transitivity of relations of equality).

Even in the face of the concrete observation of objects which he handles, until eleven or twelve years of age he will deny this conclusion which is evident to us. For example, if we take three bottles or glass jars of different forms but the same capacity, and make him decant bottle B into bottle A, he will immediately ascertain that the capacities of A and B are equal. Now if we let him decant B in C, he will ascertain without further difficulty the equality of the capacities of B and C.

But if we then ask him whether A and C have the same capacity, or a different capacity, he will be unable to reply, without decanting A into C, and will most often say: "we cannot know" or "we must try it!"

To sum up, it is around nine or ten that the child's thought evolves from transductive or analogical reasoning ("it's like") and from the juxtaposition of concepts ("and so," "and then"), to deductive reasoning ("now . . . therefore") and the logical interdependence of concepts ("because").

But it is only after eleven, twelve or thirteen—according to the difficulty of the problem—that the child is capable of coordinating an ensemble of multiple relations. He could do so as a beginning in simple and concrete problems which he will resolve by direct handling and observation. Later on, around the age of thirteen, he will go on to abstract problems of pure thought.

The experimental conclusions of the physical sciences have no probative force for the child below eleven or twelve, since he is not capable of coordinating observed facts and abstracting from them the certainty of stable and real (although invisible) relations. The logical conclusions of the mathematical sciences and the abstract explanations of arithmetical problems are on the average not accessible before the age of twelve or thirteen.

Each person can draw the evident conclusion from these facts. Our teaching of arithmetic, for example, is still too logical; it must be acted out and manipulated, for it is through action and concrete observation that the concept enters the child's mind.

The *critical sense,* the converse of logical reasoning, appears at the same time. The ten- or eleven-year-old becomes less credulous; he learns to judge what he sees, hears and says. Around the age of twelve he will often even make abusive use of this gift and begin to "cavil" and dispute everything. This will herald new difficulties with his environment.

It should be noted that this age between ten and twelve is the time when "false individuals" are formed, persons totally incapable of offering a reasonable judgment and grasping their error in a more or less restricted sphere.

5. Accurate notion of time and speed

The notions of duration, simultaneity or succession can be put forth as examples of this slow psychological maturation between the ages of five and twelve. It is significant to observe, for example, the habitual response of a six-year-old to the following:

"How many minutes do you take to go home from school?"

"Ten minutes."

"If you run, do you go faster or slower?"

"Faster."

"So, do you take more time or less time?"

"More time."

"How much?"

"More than ten minutes!"[10]

As shown by the example, the child under six does not succeed in grasping the inverse relation between duration and speed (more speed-less time). And when he does grasp this inversion around the age of six, we are even more astonished to discover that before seven or eight the child cannot understand that several visible phenomena are connected by one single duration, one single time span. Two closely synchronized actions—whose identical beginning and end he has affirmed—are not necessarily of the same duration for him.

There is a time for each of these two actions and these two durations are not comparable to each other. In general, the child judges the duration by the vague feeling he has of a more or less great effort required by the action. Hence, when water from one jar is poured into another identical jar (synchronism of the inverse two movements of the level of the water in the communicating jars), he readily affirms that the water of the lower jar took more time to reach its level, because one level rises while the other goes down (which is easier).

Similarly, before seven the child's drawings juxtapose not only objects as they are (and not as we see them: transparent houses, for example), but they even transpose scenes which would be successive and not simultaneous as far as time was concerned. This stems from a failure to perceive the relations of succession

---

10 J. Piaget, *Le developpement de la notion de temps* (Paris: Presses Universitaires, 1946).

clearly and reproduce them logically. His drawings like his stories are filled with incoherences, and do not admit of any order followed, any chronological or causal connection. It is a juxtaposition of the flow of the story and not a correlation of the facts.

Only in the neighborhod of eight or nine years of age will the child become capable of no longer confusing duration with the space traveled (*farther* in space does not always mean *after* in time); he will also be able to control durations through observation of successions or simultaneities (the two movements have stopped together or one after the other); and he will grasp the fact that in two synchronized movements a partial duration of one is shorter than the total duration of the other (the temporal junction of the part into the whole).

These mental operations surpass the possibilities of an eight-year-old; they require a good grasp of the relations of causality which little children do not have. The fine coordination of simple temporal relations is one of the great intellectual acquisitions of the ninth year. Teachers must not ignore this in the face of scholastic difficulties of children of this age or younger!

6. Objective interests

The previous period (from four to seven) had been the period of interests referred to as subjective, in the sense that the child embraced external sensorial contributions without personal control and followed the impulse of his momentary and unconscious interests. His major work consisted in focusing his sensorial and motor functions on contact with objects of the concrete world. These had scarcely any other usefulness than to act as a pretext for new activities: before seven what counts is the act, not knowledge of the object used.

From eight or nine years onward, on the contrary, objects acquire an interest for themselves; the child turns toward an effective *"grasp"* of his environment. His horizon is considerably enlarged, since the child feels capable of opening windows on time and space. He applies himself to things for themselves out of intellectual curiosity. This is the period of *objective interests*.

In his forward march, the child becomes more desirous of tangible results, and less anxious for fulfillments that are purely imaginative. This is the period of *collections*. This taste should be developed on condition that it opens the child up: to restrict his interest to vignettes of chocolate or to toys would mean to make him too narrow. This is also the period of intelligent constructive games and mechanical destructions (alarm clocks, spring engines, etc.).

We must also note an evident *eclipse of the imagination* from nine to twelve years of age, owing in large measure to the lack of fantasy in school work. We must be careful not to let it be stamped out; the same holds true for curiosity. But curiosity should normally remain more lively than imagination, by reason of the growing taste for the observable real, for experimentation and for objects rather than dreams.

This decline of the imagination is normal before the appearance of the critical sense, objectivity and logic. The teacher's task lies possibly in preserving the creative imagination which will allow the richness of verbal or artistic expression.

But his task is also to foster the advent of objectivity and adult intellectual functions. It would be dangerous for the child if the teacher keeps him in the state of credulity, fantasy and infantile forms of thought, when he should on the contrary direct him toward a normal evolution into adult thought.

The Fine Art of Teaching

We must always do the impossible so that a boy will not be catalogued as a *dunce for life* in the way that others have themselves enrolled as life members in their bowling league.

We must give him another chance to shine which might not exist through his signal lack of ability—without this he might someday become proud and boast of this very inability.

We can follow the example of their good sense. Have you never seen their art of measuring each person according to his value? And the judicious choice they make, in their circle, of leaders and roles? Therefore, we should not treat them as a herd but should entrust each one with the task which will rouse his enthusiasm.

If you do not want to cultivate egoism in this child, take care that this school rivalry does not awaken jealousy and the desire to dominate at all costs! Do you not see that this system of classifications and places encourages the child to battle pitilessly and destroys all desire for mutual aid?

Hence, instead of tempting him to beat out his friends, accustom him *to conquer himself*. Let him look upon his grades as a means of seeing not whether he can surpass others but whether he can surpass himself; whether he has made progress this week over last, whether he has taken a step forward or backward. And encourage loyal mutual aid and explanations among friends—which is much different from copying and "cheating."

Once a climate of confidence and mutual aid has been established, why not give all the children a part of autonomy which, arising from themselves, will expand their judgment, affirm their personality and perfect their sense of responsibility. Why not strive progressively for that educational ideal—which is the organization of the class by the children?

This entails, first, the class organization of discipline and the material framework, and then the organization of the work. It does not constitute the abdication of the teacher but, very much to the contrary, the multiplication of his influence and educational authority by the complete confidence and full vitality of twenty-five children!

Beginnings of social life

The real discovery of other children and the social sphere takes place around the seventh year, in the street and above all at school. It is easy to verify the social retardation, awkwardness in public and lack of know-how on the part of children who have not played with friends between seven and twelve, especially those who have started school late. In this respect, only-children from middle-class environments, or children of isolated farms far from towns are clearly at a disadvantage because of their lack of social contacts.

We come back once again to the pitfalls of social life at its beginnings. We have seen how an emotional conflict could arise and be reabsorbed in the·family circle. We will also see the possibilities for complexes in school life and in the relations of children with one another.

It is very important for a teacher to have a basic understanding of these mental phenomena, so that he can overcome them and enable numerous children to have a normal and no longer inhibited social life. In the case of most children, these are benign evils that will disappear when they are shown a little attention. But we must be careful to compensate ultimately for the sometimes stultifying influence of the family or school atmosphere which would render these difficulties durable and deep-seated.

We must be very conscious that starting school is a violent emotional shock: the child suddenly becomes one among equals. He no longer has the right to any affection except the very divided affection of the teacher, which is mitigated even more by disciplinary severities!

Commands are no longer directed solely to his person but become collective: a mother of a large family does not address herself to any of her children in the same manner, for the principal reason that they are not of the same age or possibilities.

At school, everyone must do almost the same thing and receives anonymous commands. This new fact often brings about a decline of the child's emotional manifestations in regard to his parents. Since he is no longer in permanent touch with his mother's affection, feels less loved, and moreover, loved very differently at school (this is not an evil but a simple fact), the child diminishes his marks of affection to the same extent: receiving less, he gives less.

We can also see in the moral crisis already mentioned above one of the principal reasons for this decline of emotional exuberance toward his parents. They are no longer the "good giants," perfect and all-powerful, as the child implicitly thought of them in the preceding years.

Under these circumstances, the child's social life can be manifested in three ways:

1) as *normal,* it will gradually expand the child while integrating him into the community in which he will live;

2) as *difficult,* it will more or less run afoul of the parental or scholastic powers, but after a few crises will rediscover a new equilibrium by compensation: discovering possibilities to excel in some sphere or other, the child will gradually lose his attitude of inferiority;

3) as *inhibited,* it will be restrained by persistent conflicts with the environment and in extreme cases will be able to provoke the child's turning into himself— a return to intellectual egocentrism and social isolation.

1. Normal, expanded social life

Possibly the child's most complex learning process between nine and twelve is the development of sociability. It will terminate around the age of twelve in making the child an almost fully polished individual, capable of conducting himself in the best manner before every kind of interlocutor.

When dealing with adults, the child gradually becomes less capable of politeness. It would be wrong to neglect the development of that social polish which constitutes a first stage of charity and understanding. The children of our age are impolite, but this is very often the fault of the inconsistencies of language on the part of those around them or the excessively thin patience of their parents. Politeness should very quickly become—after eight or nine—as habitual as obedience.

But the learning process of social behavior in groups of children is even more useful for the general development of each. The child discovers that not all social relations are those of superior to subordinate. He himself becomes capable of influencing other children.

He moves in a true social area which is no longer unique, and the child's world is a first model of the adult society in which he must later develop. It is the sole spot where he can learn through action (and he knows only through action) the behaviors possible in a society. We can see, then, the immense acquisition made by the child who is placed among companions in an atmosphere that allows him to carry on this learning process with sufficient freedom.

The knowledge of the needs of others, of their interests and of their reactions is not handed to the child. He must himself gradually achieve such knowledge of others which he lacks, so that around the age of eight, for example, he may be able to work effectively with his companions.

The child will attain this understanding of the various social relationships first of all through *play* which entails, in this immense and hence somewhat disquieting social universe, imbibing stable traditions and not very numerous behaviors. Coming from a family or school horizon in which the relations of obedience were predominant, the child would have difficulty in finding his way in the diversity of social behaviors between equals. Hence, a refuge against such disquieting abundance and the help of very stable traditions were not accorded him by all types of playing, from the most simple to the most complex.

The child thus makes slow progress among the various collective sports. Little schoolyard games, simple and easy to repeat, become necessary for his happiness around the age of eight or nine, and the more elaborate games around the age of ten. The more complicated woodland sports and Indian or medieval adventures will be fully tasted only around eleven, an age which sees the reappearance of imagination as well as the appearance of an interest in chivalrous heroes.

The initial *clubs* appear, at first simple gatherings of neighborhood children (five or six children about nine years or so) to play marbles or hopscotch together. There is as yet no leader among them, except at times for a clown or buffoon who dazzles them with his daring and his antics; but they have no organization, no purpose and no fixed occupations. It is a band of the neighborhood.

The time around ten, eleven or twelve constitutes the best age for gangs that generally include anywhere from six to twelve children led by a boy with leadership qualities (and persuasive biceps). The gang *arranges* fights or the epic battle with a rival gang (instincts of struggle and combat).

Whether it is through the collective games or the gang, one of the social dimensions of this age is that of the *rule* which becomes something else than a law inspired externally by an adult. True, the rules of the games are inspired by tradition and their observance is closely checked by the players or the referee. But a person is at least free to be heard in order to add a rule or modify another. He agrees on a signal, a boundary line on the field and to such conditions as are necessary to insure victory. And these agreements then have the force of law: the rule is formulated in common! What a distance this is from simple obedience to the adult rule!

It would be impossible to encourage too strongly this passage from obligatory rule to a rule that is both desired and embraced. This feeling of freedom within the framework of rules freely chosen is at the root of the acquisition of autonomy. This powerful factor of personal expansion provides the basis for the *active method of education.*

A child cannot be kept bound to obedience and dependence until he is twenty. Some day or other he must be set free and his feeling of duty, law and rule must no longer be inspired by the authority of parents (as is suitable until the age of ten) but by a personal, free and voluntary choice (as is normal around the age of sixteen or seventeen).

Such a passage must not be an abrupt one, for the child will lose his footing if all authority should collapse at once. But it must be prepared for, followed up and facilitated, progressively and prudently, over the years from nine to seventeen.

The child should be urged to make his own law, in simple cases at first, and then little by little in more complex situations. The support of our authority will never be lacking to him, but it will be imposed less and less in order to make room for progressively greater autonomy.

It is this progressive autonomy that is sought at school and in the home by the active methods that have been so warmly praised or so vehemently condemned. We see the absolute need for them as well as for the prudence that must govern their use.

While waiting for these methods to be imposed out of ordinary good sense, fortunately the child can obtain a first experience of autonomy in the infantile group: recreation periods, public squares and gardens, and especially educational groupings and children's movements.

In short, the normal child between nine and twelve must integrate himself painlessly into the collectivity, first of children and then gradually of adults. He must take an active, voluntary, joyous and free part in the collective life of children in his age bracket. This is necessary for his intellectual, emotional and moral well-being.

Formerly, the misdeeds of oppressive parents and disciplinary boarding-schools were too numerous to be counted. In our day, the excess would be in the opposite extreme—lack of authority. But there are still many families which—without returning to the inflexibility of the head-of-the-household of the past—continue to retain an attitude of brooding hens toward their young. In the laudable intention of sheltering the child from possible corrupting influences, he is kept at home, not without gorging him and making things worse in other ways often beyond measure.

Thus, whenever parents have preferred keeping their children tied to their apron strings rather than giving them supervised freedom in the yard, the result has always been a retardation (sometimes very notable) in social acquisitions. We can cite, for example, the enormous difference under this sole aspect between middle-class children and street urchins. There is also analogous harm when parents send the child to the movies or the museum, or to Aunt Suzie. There are not enough social contacts in this case and the child remains awkward in public, "backward" before the slightest progress as in games with his companions.

It is most necessary for the child that the parents understand that school plays a very great role not only as regards instruction but also as regards character formation and social adaptation. There are a good many criticisms that could be leveled at the traditional passive methods of instruction or discipline. However, on the one hand, we see evidence that the teaching profession is turning more and more to active methods (together with official reforms in courses); and, on the other hand, it would be a much graver disaster for the child if parents were to seize these deficiencies of the school as a pretext for keeping him at home for a longer time. This would constitute a grave disturbance in the socialization of the child and a retardation of his intellectual and character development.

2. Family and School Conflicts

From nine to twelve years of age, the child is at a happy age, an age without histories. Normally, he has the task of integrating himself in an infantile social world which accords him the possibility of relative autonomy.

But he can encounter difficulties in this process,

either in the family circle or at school or among companions. We will not emphasize the symptoms of these social conflicts which we have mentioned in connection with the crisis of the age of seven. As at the time after every crisis of growth, the child opposes his environment which prevents him from expanding and to that extent prolongs the crisis. We have seen what this was when the harm came from the family; the external manifestations are analogous when the bruises stem from school or companions.

Against those who hurt him the child exhibits an attitude of reflex inhibition difficult to overcome: actions of flight sometimes physical (detour by the neighboring street), sometimes only intellectual (refuge "in the moon") or emotional (apparent insensitivity, isolation); actions of taking refuge, liquefaction of physical faculties (legs "like jelly") or mental ones (impossibility of joining three words logically together) and even momentary clouding of the moral sense.

Without necessarily always leading to this grave condition, the existence of an inferiority complex inevitably hampers the systematic development of the child. It is therefore necessary to be on the lookout for it and remedy it as quickly as possible.

Outside the family, inferiority complexes are provoked by the teacher's harshness, and especially by his injustices and sarcasm. More often, the source of such complexes should be seen in the jeers of companions: concerning some physical inferiority (lisp, sickness, clumsiness or effeminacy) or intellectual inferiority in school work (rarely), in games of imagination, or in the nasty tricks that require quick thinking.

It would be impossible to give too much education and reeducation concerning charity in school circles which have until the present been condemned to egoism, to the "each-one-for-himself" philosophy, and to the triumphs of vanity through the excessively passive traditional methods and their cortege of competitive examinations, notes, gradings and rivalries. How can one possibly fail to see that such practices obstruct the learning process of sociability which is the great acquisition of this period? Instead of encouraging collaboration, we promote the most individualistic kind of competition.

The Fine Art of Teaching

Collections
> insects
> strange leaves, useful plants (medicinal, good for birds, rabbits, etc.)
> rocks, shells
> postage stamps, photos, postcards

Construction
> clay or paper maché
> wire, cardboard or construction paper
> roller skates, soap box cars
> cabins or tree houses
> taking apart and (if possible) reassembling simple mechanisms
> puppets and marionettes

Reading
> about history: great heroes of the past, epic stories, historical reconstructions
> about voyages: the great navigators, the colonial explorers, the polar seas, etc.
> about inventions

Drawing
> with crayons or watercolors on large sheets of paper, the scenes of his imagination

And if this child is bored, the fault is ours for not knowing how to help him discover all these fascinating activities over the eleven years of his life!

Delayed development
of voluntary inhibition

It is pleasant to note, and does not displease grown-ups, that nothing in the eight- or nine-year-old yet stops the surge of life: indiscreet, loquacious, restless, impolite, etc. Thus his powers are fully utilized for growth, not yet squandered by putting a brake on the riches of his vital force.

Social inhibition will later take on diverse forms: shame, human respect and concern for "what will people say?" For the moment, it is not yet fully effective and this is so much the better for the child's intellectual development, the "why's," the curiosities and the fresh spontaneity of this age.

These restraining feelings and this will for inhibition, must, however, develop bit by bit between the ages of ten and twelve. We must watch for them for it is necessary to stop the foolish impulses of the following age. But this must not destroy spontaneity!

This absence of inhibition explains—as we have said—the futility of negative orders: "Don't make any noise, don't tap your feet, don't swallow it whole without chewing," etc. Consequently, it is better to use this surge of life for strengthening the positive will which affirms itself: commands should be positive and joyous, and draw the child along.

One of the principal means of developing this will is to lead the child to overcome his fear: from ten or eleven years onward, he should be encouraged to overcome dangers to his stature and to remain calm in the face of anything that might frighten him. The little excursions into the mountains are one of these means. But the prudence and continued attention of teachers must be multiplied tenfold!

From seven onward, the child becomes capable of focusing his attention on an object for a bit longer. This attention is no longer a passive absorption of the child by the object as was formerly the case; it becomes on the contrary a voluntary action of the child who concentrates his faculties on the object in question. This blossoming of voluntary attention makes possible the child's entrance into school and the performance of the school work that follows.

But in the beginning we can expect only inhibitions of very short duration, which will gradually become easier through frequent exercise. We must not forget that the child has enormous difficulty in maintaining his attention for the full part of an hour of class: the best ten-year-old pupils are distracted at least half of the time and remember the lesson only because of the numerous repetitions of the teacher grasped in random bits and pieces. Many teachers abuse this capacity for attention by demanding a supplementary effort of lessons and overly important duties after long hours of class.

A ten-year-old should not be kept immobile for more than four hours a day. The inhibiting will is effective only at the end of adolescence, around the age of eighteen at the minimum, when the young man is fully capable of mastering his motor impulses, achieving emotional stability and disciplining his attention. This very necessary evolution to the well being of an adult requires a preparation from the tenth year onward.

Emotionality and moral sense

The emotional reactions of this age are simpler and crustier than those of the preceding age.

Between eight and twelve years of age, the child

(as has been mentioned) undergoes a partial eclipse of emotionality as well as imagination—at least, the child who is free of all complexes. This eclipse stems in part from the coldness of the school environment and also from the relative equilibrium of the child of this age, an equilibrium that is normally devoid of shocks and conflicts which would stimulate his emotionality.

Consequently, there are *great differences* among children. There are some whose emotional growth in favorable circumstances has led to a robust and expanded equilibrium. These are a bit violent, frank, active and full of health. Then there are others who underwent a painful social crisis around the age of seven and have more or less gradually "liquidated" their conflicts (or have even repressed them in themselves and retained them). These manifest a much more lively emotionality (to the slight detriment of vitality, of growth) and at times a sorry one. The latter, much more than the former, have need of an atmosphere of comprehensive affection—which does not mean affectedness or incessant overindulgence!

We must not forget, however, that if the child seems ruder and less cajoling, he always continues to need much more affection to develop. In order to live, the child needs much more love than he himself manifests externally toward those close to him.

This emotional tepidity will have repercussions on the child's religious sentiment. The child of this age no longer has merely a religion that is felt, imagined, dreamt of, and based on friendships with the Child Jesus; he gradually moves up to a religion that is intellectually grasped. Beginning with the age of eleven, the child's attention is focused on the inadequacies of a catechism which does not always leave room, on the one hand, for objections against the Christian life (in conjunction with the development of the critical sense) and, on the other hand, for the carrying out of the moral precepts in concrete daily living.

The eleven-year-old is more than ever needful of a solid, operative and lived religion; he will no longer be content with the beautiful dreams of his preceding years. He is too inclined to lump together the abstract dogmas of a religion which might not be lived with the myths of Santa Claus or the good fairies.

The child of this age group—about the time of First Communion—will easily lose the faith out of intellectual incomprehension of an etheral religion, unadapted to life, and out of disgust for imaginative dreams. He is all too ready to be positive and practical. Later on—around fourteen, fifteen and sixteen—he might also lose it, but more often out of reasons of the moral order, in the face of new problems. Abandoning religion is a very different thing at twelve than it is at fifteen.

We should further note the very great part between seven and twelve that must be allowed—in judging a child's action—for impulsiveness, for suggestion from external examples (inhibition is still feeble), for curiosity, for love of games and danger, for inexperience and for imagination. Certainly, these represent failings but they are part of the profound nature of the child and some of them are so necessary for his well being, that it would be wrong not to consider them very often if not as reasons for pardon, at least as extenuating circumstances.

But it is also certain that—insofar as the child advances in age—our judgments should accord "these failings" a more restricted place and extend the moral requirements to new problems that arise.

In any case, the teacher should strive to preserve

intact the sentiment for justice which is so vibrant at this age. He must also utilize and cause to vibrate the child's sensitive chords: desire to get big, to surpass himself, to be understood, to give pleasure, to render service, to be useful; and also love for himself.

These chords will vary from child to child: they will allow the application to each of the encouragement which all children essentially need for their moral growth. Encouragement and congratulations (the latter administered in private and not in public) are much more useful and effective for the child's moral progress than all the reprimands which we are used to heaping on him.

The Fine Art of Teaching

There is nothing worse to kill a child's respect for himself and others than the anonymity of a number or the irony of a nickname; the passivity of changes of places in rank, with arms folded; the sheeplike habit of recitations in common, distracted and badly understood; the merciless criticism of sloppy uniforms, etc. These are all plagues which still rage in a good many so-called educational institutions.

A child who does not play is sick. Have him examined by a doctor who specializes in children. A glandular treatment often puts an end to such apathy. But also seek to discover whether there may be other reasons for this: whether his companions bully him as the weakest among them, or whether they hurt him by their continual ridicule.

Furthermore, seek to discover whether behind all this there lies some great chagrin or major shock which would have sapped his strength (death of his mother, his father's remarriage, etc.). In all cases, your role is to restore his social place to this "misfit." Do not force him to mingle immediately with companions who hurt him: give him a few responsibilities and become his friend. Little by little, in once again becoming conscious of his usefulness and capabilities, he will take up his place anew, if we know how to help him.

If you are accorded the singular honor to be admitted into a gang, above all never become its head: you are only an invited guest. Be the one who "gets everything going again" by his astuteness or his influence, practice *fair play* more than ever, and do not attempt to reform the rule: how can you as a novice think of grasping the subtle intentions that brought about its formation? Merely try to be the most adept at marble-playing or sling-shooting. This is not so easy. As for the rest, you will see later on.

THE CRISIS
OF THE
AGE OF TWELVE

Third step toward autonomy

The lengthy crisis of adolescent psychology, from the age of twelve to seventeen, is not a continual one. It offers phases of calm and recrudescence. The most notable fact is that the functions in ferment are not the same at its start as at its conclusion. *The period of prepuberty* (twelve or thirteen) constitutes above all a *third crisis of opposition and social emancipation,* corresponding to the preceding ones. It is principally provoked by the development of the intellectual functions acquired between the ages of eight and twelve and allowing for a higher degree of mental autonomy.

The *period from fourteen to seventeen,* which constitutes adolescence properly so-called, will be chiefly a crisis of *physiological growth,* a *moral crisis* and an *emotional crisis.* But it goes without saying that there is no clear boundary between these two episodes, no more than between the symptoms which characterize them.

The age limits here indicated for the young man are—even more than in the case of the preceding stages—susceptible of considerable variations. Factors of precocity are: the Mediterranean climate, hot weather, city atmosphere, nervousness, freedom accorded the child, frequency of his social contacts, promiscuity and poverty. Factors of retardation are: the cold weather of mountain and nordic climes, the calm atmosphere of a nonexcited environment, the isolation of the child, his lack of autonomy, and a happy growth.

Around the age of eleven or twelve, the child goes through a period of development in all fields.

From the physical aspect, although the child has not yet reached his figure of a man, he does have a body that is well-balanced, capable of serving him perfectly through its power, suppleness, speed, the precision of its sensory-motor connections and his reserve energy.

From the intellectual aspect, the child's mind is beginning to be capable of all the intellectual operations. When he is about twelve or thirteen, he becomes permeable to the abstract and his interest extends to ideas. His judgment—provided he has gradually lost his egocentrism—has come in contact with the judgment of others and has taken on at least a rectitude which is highly variable from that of his environment, if not a personal character.

The child has discovered that one subject can give rise to very different opinions and he readily exercises his critical sense in regard to certain of these opinions when their proponent is within reach.

His *will* also serves him better and renders him capable of behaving in a way more in conformity with the rules of those around him. He feels more at ease in the various social contexts which he has learned to know little by little.

As a result of all this, the child suddenly realizes with some awe that he is as capable as others to fly with his own wings.

Possibly, this is an illusion; for although the machinery is almost ready to go, it still lacks the habit of turning the motor by itself, the experience capable of setting the judgment aright. But we must beware of clipping his wings, or of showing him his illusion, for it is necessary and even indispensable that he try his hand at the sport of life. Each individual forges his own experience.

Thus the child somewhat harshly proclaims himself capable of walking alone and refuses the help or the presence of his parents who are a little bewildered by the suddenness of this blow. For this desire for freedom often becomes magnified. The child sulks when he is made to feel the adult's superiority: he does not like it.

For a long time he has already refused his mother's hand and he sulks during the family's walks on Sunday, looking with some pity on the enthusiasm or the docility of the "little tykes." But this does not prevent him from desiring to do the same, from getting pins and needles in his arms and legs and docilely following his parents if some event gets the better of him and frightens him.

In short, *the child accepts being led by the nose* in every eventuality of drowning, *but on condition that the string is long and above all invisible*. This constitutes one of the characteristics of the social crisis of prepuberty.

The child's principal desire is to break with the past. He is no longer a little child and does not want the same clothes (the first pair of trousers!), the same books, the same teachers or leaders or the same laws.

It is only just though that he accept the same parents—but solely on condition that they no longer treat him like a little child!

Obviously, each child's personality will contribute a good many nuances to these impetuous "forces." Many children—above all those from the middle class and "only-children"—will undergo at this age only a very peaceful evolution and will very quietly do as they please, without pains and without pranks. Others will experience no crisis at all.

But a boy's personality will be truly virile only if he has achieved his autonomy at the cost of a real struggle. An opening does not occur without a rent of some kind; an adolescence that is too easy does not mold a man.

These tadpoles who do not succeed in becoming frogs are somewhat disturbing! We must distrust ourselves, that is, we must prompt the child to assume initiatives, freedom, autonomy and responsibilities, if we do not want to see a sudden explosion when he reaches the age of fifteen to nineteen—such an explosion will be all the more violent to the extent that *it occurs so late,* and so much the more hostile to the extent that a misunderstood maternal love will have tied him to its apron strings.

Normally, this crisis of emancipation appears around the age of twelve, and becomes stronger around fifteen. At this age, freedom must be conscious and discipline agreed to—but this does not yet mean that the will is capable of mastering everything.

We must insist once more on this fact: to the extent that the adolescent has failed to take progressively —in favor of each crisis between twelve and twenty years of age—the freedoms which could be normal to each age, to that same extent in which this emancipation has been retarded will the crises of opposition be more violent and at times lead to a bitter break. The teacher must *facilitate this progressive emancipation*.

Finally we should also remember that throughout this crisis of opposition, and subsequent to the violence itself of its recrudescences and lulls, the social conflicts will cause the *inferiority complexes* from the previous crises to reappear. It is at all costs necessary for the child to free himself once and for all from these complexes; otherwise, he will be shackled for life.

Adolescence constitutes the final reprieve for this freedom; hence, it is a question of placing everything in motion so that the child will be delivered from this restraint.

The child will naturally find compensation in a *superiority in some other field*. We have seen what this might be, in a family circle, for the youngest child (pp. 76-82). Although they are necessary for the child to be cured (a complex is a wound that takes a long time to heal), these compensations are often difficult to reconcile with good moral balance.

a. Weaker in body than his companions of the same age, the child will beat smaller children unmercifully and show off before them. This is the danger of *cruelty*.

b. He will split himself into several more or less fictitious persons unaware of one another: son, brother, schoolboy, companion, etc. This is the danger of the *split personality*.

c. There is also the danger of *masquerade:* the child will acquire the habit of showing himself to all under a different aspect of reality. He will play a role before everyone, and show himself as he is only to those whom he truly loves. This is a source of endless falsehoods, which are conscious to some degree.

d. There is the further danger of *mythomania:* the habit of living continually in fiction—as the leader of a gang of thieves or the king of the movies, etc.

e. Finally, there is the danger of compensation by *strife:* too often this is the revenge of those who are misunderstood or of the weak against the strong.

But, fortunately, the possible compensations are not at all harmful:

a. superiority in a branch of scholastic knowledge: geography, mathematics, etc.;

b. manual superiority: drawing, pottery;

c. superiority in recreation: games, wrestling, gymnastics (this compensation is a bit dangerous if the inferiority is intellectual: the child acquires the habit of neglecting that part of the mind and becomes a sporting enthusiast for mindless biceps);

d. protection of a younger child entrusted to him. Under this aspect, use can be made of the classes in which various ages are mixed together and in which permanent active methods are used and favor loyal mutual help.

It is our task, then, to orient this child toward those activities which will make him forget his inferiority in some other respect. What we must realize is that some kind of compensation is absolutely necessary —and it is easy to find—if we do not want the child to remain morally indigent all his life.

How many children, secretly hurt by being perpetually at the bottom of their class, have made up (compensated) for this by acquiring a solid reputation as rowdies or "terrors-in-the-gym." We must do our best to see that this compensation is useful for life: manual skill, social service, etc.

At any rate, no matter what the age, the appearance of an inferiority complex is explained only by a lack of affection and encouragement. The complex will disappear only if we help the child succeed and conquer where he can, courageously. Thus, the gradual integration of the child into his environment will take place and this should normally lead from his dependence as a baby to his freedom as a man.

All these characteristics of the age of twelve to fourteen make this period an ideal age for the education of freedom and "self-conduct." Far from disturbing the child's equilibrium this crisis of emancipation of prepuberty must *render it more solid in order to conquer the difficulties of puberty, because he is more capable of behaving himself.*

In what concerns the social development of this age, the gang instinct follows—in those who are easily sociable—a double evolution:

On the one hand, the gang around the age of twelve, takes on extension. In an urban environment this is the splendid period of "mafias" composed of anywhere from ten to twenty-five boys aged twelve to fifteen, under a competent leader who affirms himself no longer solely through his biceps but through his age, his resourcefulness and his experience of "hard knocks." It is sometimes a gang organized for shoplifting or trading goods. Each has his place and a well-defined role to play. The discipline is pitiless.

The purposes of the gang will not, however, be solely gangsterism but also bicycle jaunts, swimming and movies, yet always with a marked preference for whatever puts them outside social laws. In this way, they hope to affirm their collective personality, just as they seek to affirm themselves individually by their vanity, their desire to show off, or by their low-down tricks (crisis of originality of adolescence and susceptibility).

But on the other hand, to the extent that this gang takes on more extension and the ages become more varied, the need for affection finds less satisfaction therein. This accounts for the appearance—around the age of thirteen or fourteen—of the small group of inseparable buddies in which true *friendship* is born.

They will meet to do everything and nothing, but no longer to "swagger" and "kick up a fuss" as in a gang. And the group is established more and more for the profit of the more stable "pairs of friends."

No matter what preference the child might have for the small group or the large gang, the extreme sociability of the twelfth or thirteenth years of age is to be utilized and channeled into a common pursuit. This is the right age for educational groupings and movements of children which, if they could adapt themselves to the evolution of each child would be one of the most stabilizing factors for the *first* years of adolescence.

The Fine Art of Teaching

We must never forget that the purpose of education is to teach the child to do without us, to do without his teachers.

The art of the teacher, in short, consists in parceling out to each child the amount of autonomy that he can bear. If we allow the child that amount of freedom to which he is entitled at each age, he will not be tempted to make fraudulent use of it behind our back.

From the individual to personality, there is the same path as from the collectivity to the community or, if you prefer, from the herd to the team. All our efforts as teachers have only one purpose: to lead the child from one to the other, from a being isolated in a world which he does not know to the man who is free to render better service.

It also entails leading a class or a troop from sheeplike and passive anonymity to the *Cooperative Enterprise of the Discovery of the World and Social Utility*. Put this in capital letters if you will. And if this title displeases you as a social reason for your school—I grant you that it is quite scandalous—at least retain the idea, and in conjunction with your children build a more united world, a world in which people help instead of kill one another.

And if you break out in an incredulous and blasé smile, go get your slippers and your newspaper and sink into your easy chair! You no longer deserve these children who look to you for a spark, enthusiasm, an ideal inspiration, and a faith to move mountains.

ADOLESCENCE FROM FOURTEEN TO EIGHTEEN

The progressive emancipation of the youth between twelve and twenty would doubtless have continued if certain new factors had not made their appearance around the age of thirteen-and-a-half or fourteen. These factors disturbed this evolution, increasing other more or less violent manifestations which bewilder parents and teachers who have not been alerted.

At this age, indeed, difficulties of the social order are superimposed by other problems of the physiological, emotional and, principally, moral order. We will deal with them in turn and seek to gauge the part they play in the instability and imbalance which are the essential characteristic of this age.

An approximate idea of this superimposition (which varies greatly with individuals) of evolutive crises in the psyche of the *youth* will be given by the chart on p. 130.

The curve marked B symbolizes the consequence: a general instability so much more profound in proportion as the factors involved are more numerous (maximum between fourteen and fifteen years of age) and as imbalances are tacked on.

The crisis of adolescence is, in the highest degree, a crisis of lack of adaptation. The child was adapted to his child life in his family and school circle, with a body which served him well and an intelligence that sufficed for him; the adult will be adapted to his adult world; but the adolescent is a misfit on all levels: organic, mental and social.

In the face of possibilities which his growth produces for the adolescent, he experiences a great need to break with the past. He desires to break with his entire previous acquisition and refashion himself into a new personality who will be the adjusted man of tomorrow.

To the divorce between his physical possibilities and his love of sports, between his most solid thought and his powerlessness to act, and between his need to love and his flight into the recesses of his timidity, the adolescent opposes—over the entire course of these painful years—a great effort at unification and a violent effort at adaptation.

For he is aware of his instability, and this awareness of his weakness only aggravates this imbalance of the child and of the adult who coexist in him without being able to be harmonized by a gradual progress. Thus, we could say that adolescence is the age of "abrupt mutations." We will see what there is in the principal functions of this personality in gestation.[11]

---

[11] The purpose of this little volume is limited above all to the explanation of the psychology of the *grade school child* (seven to fourteen), we will give here only a sketch of the psychology of adolescence, as a kind of epilogue of the preceding periods.

The Fine Art of Teaching

Only in a common spirit of discovery, with an insatiable curiosity stemming from respect and admiration for a creation ceaselessly renewed, will we lead the child to the discovery of the world in which he lives. And in this way we ourselves will go on to the discovery of the heart of the child, and go on with him to the discovery of an ideal which will enthrall our youth and lead us toward an identical Star. For it is really our youthfulness of heart which will give him this mentality of an explorer and a discoverer of miracles.

Do we know how to keep a watch over this child? We should give him—as to each of the little ones—all the attention he needs. May there never be an anonymous head lost in the crowd.

Our intuition as teachers should be ardently applied and unerringly detect this personality which is beginning to bloom, to discover the birth of its interests, its gifts and its tastes. In this way, we place it without harm in favorable conditions which will enable all these new powers of the child to develop and fructify.

A school must possess the spirit of discovery which refuses to dispense knowledge in a cut and dried manner and to cram it in by force as one shoves down food. It must possess that spirit of discovery which desires to give each child his *full* opportunity to develop *all* his gifts on contact with Life.

A school must possess the spirit of discovery which enables every child to walk on his own two feet in his avid quest for knowledge and science. It must possess that spirit of discovery which enables every child to look upon the wonders of an unknown world with his own eyes rather than with the expressionless and jaded eye of that anonymous monster which is the Student-type!

The teacher must possess the spirit of discovery which refuses to plunge the child into a system of regimentation that he has neither formulated nor accepted; which refuses to drown the child in a routine of external practices that he has neither understood nor assimilated. The teacher must possess that spirit of discovery which refuses to furnish a ready-made ideal in three easy lessons learnedly composed to the rhythm of past ages, but completely unsuited to the present time, to the age and personality of this particular child.

Physical development

The chief change of this period takes place in the physical sphere. In practice, it will condition all the other evolutions of this age. This growth does not take place simultaneously in the case of all organs.

1. First, there is an *elongation of the bones,* from the age of twelve-and-a-half onward, and sometimes late (fourteen or fifteen). This very rapid growth in stature can bring on physiological troubles of a more or less grave character: tuberculosis of the bones, deformation of the spinal cord, muscular cramps; these last two phenomena are the result of weakness of the muscles.

2. The *muscles* painfully follow this elongation and lose their power. The boy is a real "daddy-long-legs": long arms and long legs that he does now know what to do with. The trunk grows much less quickly than the members.

3. Since the *enlargement of the thorax* clearly occurs later (around the age of fifteen), the youth suffers from this imbalance: insufficient respiration, and lung fatigue.

4. The *heart* also develops with a certain delay over the frame and muscles; this leads to heart fatigue which is so frequent at this age: hypertrophy, tachycardia, and circulatory troubles (cyanosis of the extremities).

5. *Maturation*—at very variable times between fourteen and seventeen—*of the sexual organs.* Preliminary extension of the pilose system and voice-change. This represents a considerable stage in glandular development; it is accompanied by a new muscular equilibrium. All the glands with internal secretion are involved in this transformation: their intimate inter-

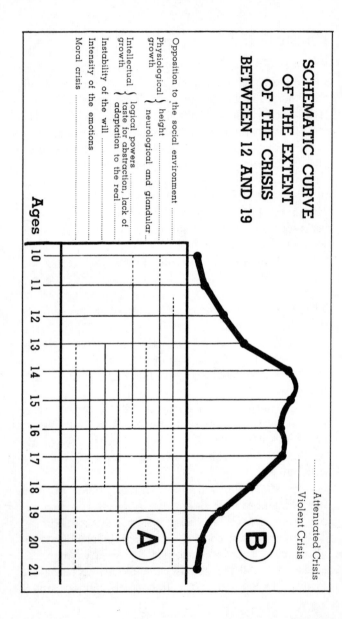

SCHEMATIC CURVE OF THE EXTENT OF THE CRISIS BETWEEN 12 AND 19

Opposition to the social environment ....

Physiological } height ....
growth } neurological and glandular ....

Intellectual } logical powers ....
} taste for abstraction, lack of ....
growth } adaptation to the real ....

Instability of the will ....

Intensity of the emotions ....

Moral crisis ....

Ages

.... Attenuated Crisis
—————— Violent Crisis

10 11 12 13 14 15 16 17 18 19 20 21

A

B

resonance lies at the source of a good many retardations of growth or profound imbalances. In a general manner, puberty (in the exact sense of the word, that is, the maturity of the sexual organs) marks the end of the physiological crisis.

This considerable evolution has as its result:

1. A diminished general resistance: sensitivity to microbial infections.[12]

2. Less muscular resistance, especially around thirteen or fourteen when the child would like to ask a greater effort from his body for the sake of his desires. Competitive sports are a real danger between thirteen and sixteen: one can never warn teachers, parents and children too much against "overtiredness" and all excesses of fatigue at this age. Cardiac troubles and above all very grave lung troubles can result. It is a large step from sports or exercise in the fresh air to competitive sporting matches: we must be careful not to let this step be taken too quickly.

3. Less ease of gestures. The young adolescent is often ungraceful, awkward and gross. And his clumsiness is further increased by his consciousness of it. He no longer possesses the lightness and suppleness of childhood.

4. Increasing need for a rich and balanced diet necessary for these multiple and accelerated growths. The adolescent must eat more than an adult (more even than a manual laborer). In particular, he needs an abundant ration of mineral salts for bone growth (milk, vegetables, etc.), and sugar to combat muscular fatigue.

5. Need for sleep, which is more necessary since the organism tires quickly, and harder to satisfy, since

---

[12] If the tubercular primo-infection has not produced itself around seven, it will often occur between fourteen and seventeen, but much more virulently.

the boy does not want to go to bed early "like the little children."

6. Nervous overexcitement, lack of intellectual attention, hyperemotionality, general instability.

7. Sudden attacks of fatigue: he is "beat." Gaps of the will (do not ask this boy for a continuous and prolonged effort). Memory gaps: this physical fatigue often destroys the intellectual powers to such a point that a temporary suspension of studies is sometimes necessary. The mental strain of students is very much to be feared or, more exactly, the mental strain resulting from the poor organization of the child's activities and his lack of muscular repose. Yet, this age coincides with important examinations and difficult preparations!

Intellectual development

The evolution of the intellectual faculty is considerable between twelve and seventeen years of age. It is also different in persons who cease all coherent intellectual effort around the age of fourteen and in those who pursue studies, or retain the taste for reflective observation, intelligent reading and study. Sociologists have estimated that the mean mental age of a population, even such a developed one as our own, is fixed approximately at the age of twelve. The only ones who surpass this mean are those who continue to make use of their intellectual capacities and to make every effort to use them.

It seems that we can distinguish from twelve to fourteen a *period of focusing* the last intellectual apparatus (logic, comprehension of abstract relations, etc.), and, from fourteen to eighteen and over, a *period of maturation* through the exercise of these same functions which degenerate and are lost if they are not put to use. A machine that does not run grows rusty and becomes clogged.

It is through repeated and continuous intellectual effort that the intellectual function is refined and becomes, around eighteen, capable of philosophical abstraction. Furthermore, this last capacity will offer its full development only around twenty-four or twenty-five, although other faculties, especially the memory, will no longer be capable of progress at this age.

Around the age of fourteen, at the same time that new problems appear for the moral consciousness, the youth becomes capable of introspection. He is also able to understand people better by readily entering into their mind, which the child could in no case do, other than by a vague global intuition.

We must note as a corollary of this emerging taste for abstract ideas a taste marked by mechanical or literary *invention*. The child sketches plans for a house, arranges the machinery of his mechanism more logically in his mind, on paper or on his finger tips, plays with more pleasure at writing a novel and composing a poem.

Adolescence sees the appearance and development of the *creative imagination* which contributes grist for the mill of all the tendencies of this age: love of daydreaming, desire of evasion, will to create new things by reaction against traditional ones, need for affirming oneself through originality, etc.

Together with a greater faculty to arrange ideas, there appears a wide current of interests for intellectual, social and moral values. This leads to a more lively interest in reading and experimental researches. The result is a greater socialization of thought: liking for discussions, exchanges of opinions, discovery of a world of opinions and theories which were not those of his environment.

This is a new factor of moral imbalance, so much more since the judgment—on contact with all these new thoughts—is befuddled and reels under the profusion of new and violent feelings which the will, still feeble, cannot master. It is also, for those whose family has very narrow ideas, a new source of conflicts and discussions. These are more violent in proposition as the adolescent sticks to his ideas, which he expresses without nuances and without diplomacy, and in proportion as there does not weigh on him as on his parents the weight of social conventions or habits formed. The result is a certain intellectual contempt of the adolescent for his parents whom he readily judges to be backward. He believes himself superior because he is not bound as they are by a world of propriety or routine.

Exchanges are multiplied and intellectual interest expands; but adolescent thought remains largely egocentric. His interests are directed chiefly to discoveries which closely affect his personality, which favor his evasions, and which enable him to contradict those around him. About the age of sixteen, the youth will gradually take pleasure in handling pure ideas, grand theories and paradoxes, as much out of intellectual sport as out of interest in these ideas.

Emotional phenomena and social development

During adolescence too many physiological, glandular or neurovegetative phenomena are superimposed for the emotional aspect not to experience violent repercussion, especially since it is connected to the nervous network, which in this evolution, sustains the greatest effort.

Malaises, fatigues and ardors, and new sensations force the child to pay greater attention to his body, particularly to the sexual functions. He blushes, pales, trembles, appears fearful or irascible, timid or assured, anxious or melancholy, in a very brief space of time.

We must not attach too much importance to these phenomena of short durability. The age of fourteen to seventeen marks the painful age of the "black hypocrite." An unshakeable optimism, joined to much tact and calm, on the part of the teacher, will overcome the characteristic instability of the adolescent.

The appearance of a new interest in himself and in others has caused this age to be named the *period of emotional interests.* The adolescent feeds on his feelings. Contrariwise to the child who was expansive and loudly manifested his feelings, the adolescent interiorizes his emotions and thoughts, and deliberately shelters them from foreign incursions (of either adult or companions) by the falsehood of protection or the shield of a facilely cynical irony.

In short, the adolescent frequently manifests feelings contrary to those which he really experiences. He aspires for the ideal, and platonic love, and reacts to beauty; but he will be correspondingly more gross in words and act blasé about everything.

Friendship becomes very important at this age and often takes the form of an exclusive, violent and secret feeling which he must at times expand. On the other hand, the child bears a different interest toward the other sex: first love makes its appearance. It is already late to educate the discipline of feelings, but it is still very necessary to do so.

We must also note that the vividness of the boy's

feelings at this age remains in general very platonic and idealized. This is especially true to the extent that the boy feels awkward and maladroit.

Furthermore, it depends largely on his family and social entourage whether the adolescent will retain for several more years the serene attitude of the child toward feminine coquetries. In general, it is the environment which renders the first encounters between boys and girls troubled and precocious. It is important not to place the adolescent in an atmosphere of promiscuity in which an exaggerated importance is attached to these questions.

From the angle of social development and autonomy, adolescence is a stage very diversely marked according to environments and personalities. The child, who is very cruelly plunged into professional life after high school clearly acquires a greater autonomy (which is easier accepted by parents) than the one who goes on to higher studies. The first paycheck is for the adolescent an infinitely more important event than promotion to high school.

The adolescent who continues his studies is too often still regarded as a child by the family. He remains at a school age although the other passes on to the professional age and approaches manhood. It is important that the family of the collegian or graduate student compensate for this retardation on the social plane by encouraging the young man to emancipations which will foster his development (trips, in particular).

The desire for emancipation also suffers eclipse. Either because a certain autonomy has been obtained (and must be assimilated before passing on to the following stage) or because the adolescent finds himself involved with other difficulties, he seems less demanding between fifteen-and-a-half and seventeen than he was the two previous years. But these crises are extremely different in accord with the personalities and the conditions presented by the environment.

Around seventeen, the opposition will often concern the profession chosen by the youth, and his relationships or first friendships with girls. Finally, between nineteen and twenty-two—often in favor of military service—a last crisis of emancipation will generally free the young man from his family care. He will frequently go to live under another roof, or take steps or come to an agreement with his parents for payment of room and board to preserve his complete independence. He will at last have achieved his autonomy as a man which will be developed fully only in marriage.

It is necessary that the family accept and foster this normal evolution. It is also indispensable that all previous conflicts be definitively laid to rest; otherwise, they will revive with this crisis and they are capable of inhibiting the adolescent and of embarrassing him for life. The feelings of inferiority must be counterbalanced before the youth approaches life; otherwise, he will possibly be the vaudevillian type of administration employe awkwardly twisting his hat in his hands and blushing before the object of his unrequited love!

The adolescent will always be an unfortunate and isolated being in his fear of life, unless his personality as a child was very strong and the revolt one day erupts violently. This works possibly for the child's good, since by harshly opposing himself he affirms himself and develops. But there is also a possible danger if this state of revolt persists in the adolescent and in the adult by way of an attitude of constant social opposition and always insatiable demands.

In any case, teachers will be more than ever vigilant to foster counterbalances which while wholly deriving the social tensions therefrom will bring to the adolescent a real development. We must utilize the love for the arts which emerges at this age, as well as the intellectual love for personal research and autonomous studies. Above all, we must encourage the very great capacity of this age for devoting self to a social science, or to a great work.

This is why adolescence—despite its shortcomings and instability—is the great age for *youth movements*. First, such groups foster this necessary emancipation, taking the child outside his family yet not abandoning him to his own resources. In them the adolescent finds himself free, but we as teachers—in them more than anywhere else—are in a position to complete his education.

Moreover, youth movements have the merit of interesting the adolescent in a real social effort, of making him participate in the social work of adults and developing in him the spirit of service which is so sorely lacking to our age. Hence, we must see to it that the movements to which we entrust our children are not overly confirmed in their character of "clubs" and keep alive the spirit of knowledge of which these boys are capable in their desire to be useful. An excessively closed, clannish spirit would destroy the child's social sense and altruism by fostering a narrow egoism to which the child is only too readily prone by the examples of the adult world.

We must also add that adolescence is the age of "team" spirit and it is very useful to encourage this community spirit. Youths love to roll up their sleeves and take part in a grand enterprise which is good for them and is their work. This feeling opens them up and prevents the turning within self to which certain of them are strongly inclined and influenced by the example of their environment.

Emotional complexes inadequately taken care of, primitive instincts which excite, emotional "forces" as violent in hostility as in affection, fantasies of an over-active nervous system—all this gives the present age an appearance of continual agitation. We must understand and bring home to those close to the child that these natural phenomena represent extenuating circumstances and an excuse for a good many excesses. The child is not yet in control of the profound transformation which is tearing him apart.

But we must not yet draw the child's attention to this fact, since he might then find pleasure in such states or use them as a pretext for every cowardice and weakness to which he is only too prone as it is. We must simply know how to show him from time to time he is not the "eternally misunderstood person" he thinks himself to be.

In order for this emotionality not to take pleasure in every kind of stimulant or abandonment, it must find healthy nourishment. It is the task of teachers to aid this search. The need for new affections will be directed toward sympathetic friends. The *quest for the beautiful* will be refined by the graphic arts or music: this is the lovely period of artistic flights. *The desire for effort* will be preserved by the exercise of some odd hobby (pottery, catching butterflies or some simple manual pastime); and his *curiosity*, by the collections he accumulates or his scientific inquiries. Above all, his *imagination* must be oriented. It passes through periods of sentimental evasions which should not assume exaggerated importance.

In short, amid this confusion, it is a question of

"saving one's valuables," of preserving hale and hearty the enormous possibilities of this age. The arts, poetry or simply pottery and reading could provide an excellent derivative, a suitable "sublimation," for an imagination overly inclined to a more or less unhealthy revery.

We should note, lastly, that this emotionality will also find an ennobling atmosphere in religious sentiment (this is the period of mystical "forces" and vocations) and in the service of others. Religious riches constitute an inexhaustible source for raising the child's morale and helping him in his ever painful struggles.

The Fine Art of Teaching

We must be filled with a very great respect for every living being and, with much greater reason, for every man and child. We must become humble in order to understand the child, and never cement him in a hasty and irrevocable opinion. We must be ever ready to revise our judgment of anyone and always regard each child as a little better than he is in reality. To avoid being discouraging and cold, we must be imbued with optimism and the desire for the child's progress. To be optimistic does not mean to be blind; it simply means to respect the enormous powers for progress which are contained in this child!

No amount of knowledge will suffice in this task if we have failed to fill our hearts with great faith and profound love. Faith in the considerable possibilities of each child, no matter how difficult he may be to lead. Faith in the obscure efficacy of our efforts, no matter how lost they may seem in an ocean of failures and abandonments. And nothing less than that faith in the might of the One who feeds the birds, makes the lilies of the field grow and guides children!

No amount of knowledge will suffice if we have failed to overcome man's vanity and pride by giving second thought—at each instant and for each child—to what our knowledge dictates to us in its barrenness and sterility; and also if we have failed to check our intuition with those who have toiled to rear these children before us.

If we regard ourselves as omniscient in comparison with the ignorant and infallible in comparison with the hesitant, we will never notice all the miseries which have much greater need of goodness and love than of our knowledge and intuition as teachers.

Moral crisis

In the face of all these new elements a moral crisis is almost inevitable.

On the one hand, the youth feels himself prey to new and violent appetites; new problems present themselves to his consciousness: sexual questions, more or less wholesome sympathies, desires for autonomy, etc.

On the other hand, however, his will no longer responds. It is less than ever capable of triumphantly resisting all these pressures, and we know how dependent it is on nervous instabilities and endocrine variations.

Thus we can explain the moral crisis of the age of fourteen or fifteen generally as follows: the twelve- or fourteen-year-old has deliberately cut himself off from points of solid refuge (he no longer wishes to ask help and advice from his family). But he discovers that in the first place he is still not very capable of using this freedom, lacking as he is in will power and experience; secondly, he finds that moral problems become terribly complicated at this very age when he no longer wants help.

This leads to the danger of discouragement. Adolescence must not be an age of abandonments. It has need of much encouragement and moral support, with the sole condition that these do not diminish freedom but rather strengthen it.

From the religious point of view, it is the doubting age. The faith needs to be solidly shored up on the one hand by intellectual logic (proofs of credibility) and on the other by concrete activities (services) which connect religion with the devotion of which this age is capable.

On the contrary, in his periods of euphoria the adolescent is capable of bursts of enthusiasm, considerable efforts and even fleeting heroisms. If this age could be the age of complete abandon, it is also the age of complete generosity, disinterestedness and prodigality of a superabundant vitality.

We must encourage the youth but not be too astonished at such sudden "collapses": these alternating highs and lows are physiological in origin. The important thing is to profit from the "highs" to strengthen the will and energy, to bolster the faith and the spirit of charity. At such moments we will entrust him with responsibilities of short duration, but requiring serious efforts. He must be shown *understanding and confidence,* but on his part he must also not rely too much on himself.

In short, the adolescent is characterized as follows:

1) *By a crisis of growth* in all spheres, and especially by violent growth on the physiological plane;

By a deep-seated instability stemming both from the violence of impulses and a very great propensity for getting tired;

2) In the social order, by a *systematic break* on the part of the child who repudiates the influences he had accepted until then, followed by an *effort at reintegration* into a different social sphere;

By the anxious search for a new equilibrium which has become necessary, a search which must end—under pain of mutilating the personality—in a progressive autonomy in every domain;

3) On the intellectual plane, by a partial and momentary return to an unconscious *egocentrism, a turning in on self,* which isolates the adolescent from the social world which he flees, and too often shuts him up in dreams and abstract ideas, outside the con-

cern of concrete contingencies and practical applications.

By a logic totally pervaded by feelings and an intoxication of ideas which foster partiality;

4) On the emotional plane, by a *transformation of filial affection* which becomes more reasoned and less expansive;

By an efflorescence of violent feelings which he hides as best he can under a cynical and mocking exterior;

5) On the moral plane, by a *profound crisis* resulting from the appearance of new and difficult problems for which he has never been prepared (sexual problems), but also by an intense search for the ideal and a profound admiration for personalities of high moral tone; the adolescent needs heroes;

6) On the religious plane, by a *crisis of intellectual doubt,* by an abandonment connected with the moral difficulties or on the contrary by a mystical expansion.

The Fine Art of Teaching

The love of effort is like a fragile plant that only asks to flower and grow. But we must not let it die of hunger, nor crush it beneath the weight of our skepticism. It needs much encouragement!

To encourage does not mean to substitute oneself for the child and do in his place what he does badly. To encourage does not mean to abuse or to punish. To encourage means to show the child how he can overcome the difficulty that stands in his path. It means giving him an attitude of a winner.

There are winners and there are losers. There are above all those who lose without putting up a fight. We must impart to the latter the desire for taking a risk and for fighting back. We will not achieve this from the comfort of a soft armchair, with our slippers warming our feet. Nor will we achieve it from the heights of a magisterial chair, armed with a ruler and piece of chalk. To achieve this demands that we ourselves be winners who walk ahead of the children.

And if we might fear the pride of some child, this is no reason to "shower" him with our coldness and restrain his enthusiasm. We must first show him that he is not the only winner, that there are others much more deserving than he is. Finally, there is a long way to go, a big country to conquer; in other words, his job is not finished by any means.

Then on the evening of some defeat we might possibly make him realize that nothing is really worth anything except love and charity, and the service of others. A long time afterward, we will realize what has been gained when we see him gradually give his every ounce of energy for these little and weak children whom he once looked down on, and who have so much need of his love that he makes himself a little one like them—whereas he is the strong one.

SCHEMATIC CURVE
OF MENTAL GROWTH

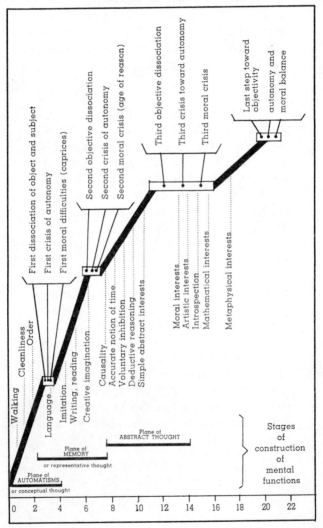

FOR BETTER
UNDERSTANDING
AND
GREATER SERVICE

After having given a very brief analysis of the characteristics of each age in the preceding pages, it may be useful to reconstruct these details in a panoramic view which will give a better understanding of the child in his complexity.

If we examine the chart on p. 148, we will gain a better understanding of the rhythms of the stages of child growth. We can therefore give a broad summary of these stages as follows:

from 0 to six months   Construction of the basic automatisms.

from 6 months to   Utilization of the automatisms.
2-3 years   Construction of the sensorial-motor functions.

from 3 to 6-7 years   Utilization of the sensorial-motor modes of thought ("manual thought").

Construction of functions associated with memory (intuition, representation).

from 7 to 12-14 years	Utilization of the modes of intuitive and representative thought.
	Construction of the functions of logical thought.
from 14 to 18 years	Utilization of the modes of logical thought.
over 18	Full utilization of the modes of concrete, intuitive and rational thought (pure science, philosophy).

The accidents of evolution

The child's mental construction is roughly analogous to that of a house. There is the upper level of relatively independent stories which are nevertheless connected by stairs, corridors, water, etc. And just as there can be no story if the ground floor is missing, so the child cannot reach the higher planes if the previous ones are not established.

Likewise, just as—at a less grave stage—a house without a cellar is less solid than a house established on strong foundations, so a mental edifice constructed on an overly narrow and not very solid "plane of automatism" is itself shaky and unstable. Mental instability —with the exception of origins resulting from nervous shocks—often stems from the inadequacies of first childhood and the sicknesses or suffering of that age.

And just as a crumbling house is taken apart starting with the roof, so mental old age is a taking apart which attacks first of all the functions acquired last. Old age follows the stages of childhood, dissolving the most recent remembrances before making the old ones disappear, and turning from altruism to egocentrism and from the future to the past and then the present.

One of the essential conclusions that can be drawn from this study seems to be the following: *the order of acquisitions can in no case be disturbed*. We can foresee in case of a deficiency in the acquisitions of a stage:

A. A delay that it is impossible completely to make up later on, when the normal period for their elaboration will have passed.

B. A very great difficulty—and, in serious cases, an absolute impossibility—in constructing the mental functions which should normally be elaborated later.

It can happen, for example, that a child has been unable to walk until the age of three and has been unable to attain all the normal acquisitions of the "plane of automatism," either because of some serious and lengthy illness or because of some congenital deficiency. It is an unfortunate probability that this child will have infinitely more difficulty first in making up this missing construction and then in laboriously rising to the following levels of: (a) manual thought and concrete behaviors, (b) representative thought and the play of imagination or memory, (c) logical thought and scholastic acquisitions, (d) abstract thought and scientific knowledge.

Every physical, mental or social factor capable of impeding mental development will leave more or less indelible traces.

Lengthy illnesses, accidents leading to some infirmity, pressures from a stifling environment, mental shocks—to the extent that such disturbances impede the acquisitions of the moment, they will leave in the personality a void not always possible to fill.

A child who is sick for a long time between the

ages of four and six will never acquire the same sureness of senses and muscle as the child who will normally have exercised his sensorial-motor connections by the sports of this age. He will not have the same love for sports.

A child who during an illness between the ages of six and eight has found sufficient food for his imagination in picture books or in his mother's stories will later have a gift for imagination as lively as and possibly more lively than that of his companions. For he will have allotted a great part of his mental energy to this occupation which was allowed him, dreams and stories, whereas active sports were not allowed him. But it is highly possible that he will resent this and never rediscover the love for hoops, balloons and tenpins which he should have had at the age of seven.

Of course, it is not a question of tenpins or balloons for themselves, but of all the functions brought into play and sustained by these, of the entire *corporal comportment* of the child, his love for *physical* effort, and his *interest in discoveries* in the world about him. We will rediscover here the essential truth that playing constitutes the child's work, his vital occupation, as indispensable for him as nourishment; without playing, the child develops badly.

Even in the case already mentioned, while admitting that his environment gives the child sufficient materials during his illness for satisfying his imagination, it is highly possible that this imagination will remain morbid for the rest of his life! Either it becomes accustomed to turn in on itself (egoism of those who have been ill for a long time) or it does not take from the external world the objective data that the child takes at this age of initial social contacts.

Thus, it frequently occurs that this *missing stage*

in the child's development leaves a notable "lack to be made up" in him and very often an incomprehension of this gift which he has not exercised. On the other hand, it is also possible and frequently happens that because of this missing stage he retains a kind of unsatisfied lifelong hunger for the particular acquisition that he missed. There remains a latent need for revenge which can seriously accentuate the general state of painful and definitive dissatisfaction that consumes certain embittered, demanding and ever insatiable individuals. A "missing stage" lies at the bottom of a good many anomalies of character.

A long illness often leaves a serious imbalance in the child's mentality because it completely destroys the normal evolutive cycle, especially from the viewpoint of character and social life. An illness places the child or the adolescent once more in strict dependence vis-a-vis his family and particularly his mother—a dependence which is no longer normal at this time.

The result is an emotional, moral and social puerilism which is disastrous although it might accompany an intellectual and physical development that is almost normal. The harmony of the development is shattered and sometimes unbalanced for a long time.

Hence, there is danger for the future well-being of the child and even the adult, if the educational atmosphere and circumstances have obstructed some stage of mental growth. *The same holds true for moral growth:* the *regularity of life habits* of the first period, the *stability of the commands and prohibitions* of the second period, and the *progressive* emancipation of the third period could be disturbed for various reasons: tenacious emotional complexes, absence of paternal firmness, absence and overstrain of the mother who works outside the home, excessive indulgences, lack of supervision, resignation of authority on the part of parents who no longer take the trouble to "lose time" with their children, who no longer have sufficient contact with them and abandon their situation as chief advisers to the profit of leaders more or less chosen from among their companions or older brothers or sisters.

A "missing stage" in the construction of the moral sense can obstruct the entire development and equilibrium of the child and the adolescent. We need not look elsewhere for the causes of a periodic recrudescence of juvenile delinquency. It is therefore accurate to say that a man's moral sense is constructed not from his youngest years but *from his earliest months.*

In the same order of ideas, it would be illusory, under the pretext of "making the child gain a year," to wish to speed up too much the slow labor of mental maturation or to attempt to disturb the normal relationships. Too many parents would like to teach their children to read beginning with the age of five or to ignore the rules and limits of age.

The adult who is too much in a hurry is the worst kind of teacher. Each new acquisition must arrive in its own time; it is most often heralded by new interests and curiosities that must be satisfied. It is the eminent role of the attentive teacher to supervise the birth of these appetites and to provide for each child at the proper time. Once it has made its appearance, this function must be exercised for a fairly long time in order to be refined and strengthened (functional exercise).

We must give it time to develop before having recourse to some other subject of effort under the pretext that "this child does not rank very high in his class and must always be given a push." Obviously! If you place knockwurst and sauerkraut before a fifteen-month-old baby, he has to be coaxed to eat. Wait then until his appetite develops for such things and give him good baby foods. This is much more true since the appetite in question will not develop for all children at the same age or period, at this same beginning of the month of September of the school year!

It is by facilitating the exercise of present functions, of the possibilities of today, that the teacher will render the acquisition of the functions of tomorrow easier. By wishing to hasten this acquisition, we only end up by *destroying in him all appetite,* all curiosity and all desire for effort. Yet precisely these gifts are the most precious of childhood! Nevertheless, this is the frequent result of interventions inspired by family or school.

There is also no less real danger on the teacher's part in wishing to slow up under the pretext of completing the recent acquisition. It is not necessary for the teacher to retard the normal evolution by delaying on one stage. For it is not necessary to seek to put the roof on a house before having constructed the ground floor; but when constructing the ground floor it is necessary to prepare the materials for the second floor which will be constructed later.

In all this the child's interests must guide the alerted teacher. The teacher will patiently observe their appearance, and will also facilitate this appearance by some "trial balloons." In any case, he must be ready to provide what the child needs for his mental health and not let him wait.

If for example, it is completely indispensable for the child to acquire very solid bases in the earliest grades (reading, writing, arithmetic), it is disastrous for him to delay over them and develop the attitude of being distracted.

The majority of children normally endowed spend too much time on these introductions, generally as a result of a faulty adaptation to the conditions of scholastic endeavor: the class is much too numerous, his interest has too many reasons for wandering, his attention is demanded for too long a time (so the student does not give it) and it is unable to be obtained for the ten or fifteen minutes which would suffice for the assimilation.

The child is placed in conditions which almost force him to "fool around"; he is made accustomed to expend no effort, and then we are astonished when at the age of nine he can scarcely read and does not suceed in adding correctly. We must entertain the child's appetite, encourage him to make progress, and give him the means for working at his pace. But the present conditions in school retard the child.

The Fine Art of Teaching

It is very desirable that his family life and the concerns of his mother allow each child to take the anatomical particularities of the other sex in stride. Likewise, it goes without saying that coeducation outside the family has its usefulness as well as its grave dangers.

Scholastic coeducation is dangerous if the child has not been prepared for it by a very solid and very precocious education for the respect of others, all living things and all creation. A child who sees nothing wrong in carving his initials in the bark of a tree or scribbling his name on walls will hardly see anything wrong in pulling girls' hair or provoking boys.

Coeducation can do fruitful work by preparing boys and girls, from childhood and without danger, for the healthy relations of normal life. It can do so by giving the widest leeway to active methods, by inculcating in each child the sense of his complementary capacities to those of his neighbor and encouraging communication between children, and by forming the sense of responsibility and rendering a just freedom to all so that they can turn their efforts toward a common purpose.

Mixed classes are most often dangerous from a moral point of view beginning with the age of eleven or twelve. And in the present state of collective instruction which has failed to adapt itself to the different individual personalities, it is awkward to impose a common didactics on different mentalities.

Intelligence quotient

It goes without saying that the indications of age given in the preceding pages are all approximate. In reality, no two personalities undergo the same learning processes at exactly the same moment.

It is understood, above all, that these indications do not have the same rigor throughout life: in proportion as the child advances in age, his development can be subject to ever greater precocities or retardations, a mental retardation of three or four months is notable at the age of two; it is negligible at the age of twelve.

This accounts for the notion—already arbitrary but all the same closer to reality—of the *intelligence quotient:* relation of the (advanced or retarded) mental age to the real fixed age; it better expresses the importance of a retardation; in the example below we have

$$IQ = \frac{\text{mental age in months}}{\text{real age in months}} = \frac{20}{24} = 0.83$$

for the two-year-old. But for the twelve-year-old:

$$IQ = \frac{140}{144} = 0.97$$

which is normal, given the imprecision of the psychological measures which do not seek to estimate a level close to two or three hundredths.

The approximate character of the indications of age are thus accentuated from birth to maturity and to old age. Before the age of ten, the *normal* variations will be spread out over several months. Adolescence shows advances or retardations of two or three years depending on the family environment and conditions of life, studies or professional labor. In the case of the adult and the old person, the stages of maturity and decline can be in advance or in retard of fifteen or twenty years!

Psychology is not the whole man

Is it necessary to add—for those who like plans all complete and work cut and dried and would thus feel cheated at not finding herein all that they need in their capacity as teachers—that psychology is only one of the sciences indispensable for the teacher? *Psychology* gives general laws to which every normal child must adhere in his mental development.

It does not remain less true that Peter, Paul and Johnny will not accomplish this development in the same manner. Yet all three of them are normal! But Peter always has a ready smile on his face; Paul is happy one day irritable the next two days; as for Johnny, he is a big "good-natural sap" who laughs with some, weeps with others and lets himself be led around by the nose.

These three boys—it can be stated in advance—will not pass from the stage of their fourteen years in the same manner. It is the subject of the *science of character* to distinguish the principal types of mentalities and to interpret in terms of these types the overly rigid laws of general psychology.

A teacher who is concerned not to cast all children into the same mold but to apply to each child the particular "finishing touch" he needs to develop—that is, a real teacher—cannot ignore at least the essential bases of the science of character which is adapting the laws of psychology to each child will enable him to dispense to each child the education suitable for him.

On the other hand, in a world disturbed by the recent war and still unstable in its security, it goes without saying that at least a general understanding of the basic laws of *biological evolution* is necessary for the teacher so that he can grasp the modes of physiological growth of any particular child: nutritional imbalances, lack of vitamins, and nervous strain are at the bottom of countless physical irregularities which the teacher must absolutely take account of in order to direct each child—*with the doctor's help*—to the effort that he can provide.

Furthermore, frequently the teacher is the only one who discovers precociously some contagious sickness or some bony deformation (curvature of the spine) to which families—out of habit—do not always pay sufficient attention.

The same is unfortunately true in the field of *mental pathology* and child psychiatry: traumatisms of war, frequent abandonments and absences, fatigue of teachers, and nervous postwar atmosphere are at the origin of *very numerous mental anomalies* upon which we have been unable to insist in the restricted limits of this work.

Moreover, we must realize that such children are extremely numerous and that about twenty or twenty-five percent *of school groups* can justifiably be submitted to serious examination by the specialists of a *medico-pedagogical Center*. Certainly, it is not a question of grave mental anomalies in the case of all; but it is a question of all without exception being submitted to a pedagogical regimen enlightened in a precise fashion by the very diverse deficiencies that can be uncovered in these centers. And this regimen adapted to each is very necessary for his present and future well-balance.

Most often it is disastrous for these children to wait until troubles are aggravated following an inadaptation to social life and school work, and until such deficiencies have become more difficult to re-educate with age. It is therefore absolutely necessary for all teachers, parents, masters and directors of educational movements in particular to be up-to-date on the principal symptoms of mental irregularities. Above all they should never hesitate to have recourse to specialists of medico-pedagogical centers when there is possible doubt about a child's suitable adaptation. This role of investigator which devolves on teachers could avoid a good many disasters.

But the teacher's knowledge cannot be limited to this. We are too prone to forget that the child is not an unreal being, independent of his environment. Peter son of a needy laborer, Jack son of an upper middle-class father, and Paul son of a longshoreman cannot re-act in the same way to life (they could not do so even if their characters were analogous), to the advice of their teachers or the solicitations of their environment. They have not been subject to the same influences from their parents, the same appeals from the street, the same development or the same deformations from their leisure time, and the same orientations of spirit or the same games from their school or their companions.

Even if a teacher has a deep knowledge of the psychology of the child in general, even if he has discerned with all the necessary refinement the particularities which make up the irreducible originality of each character, he must know—*in order for his teaching efforts to be effective*—*the influences of the life situations of the child*. This is a question of *sociology*.

Unfortunately, there are no textbooks of sociology which deal especially with this study of the influences of social groupings on childhood. This is a pity, for we must be really persuaded that a *sociology of childhood is as indispensable to the teacher as is psychology.* Especially in our day, psychological laws are too profoundly affected by social pressures to remain invariable above sociological laws.

The Fine Art of Teaching

The person who dares to assert on a particular day that he is satisfied at a task accomplished and goes off to loll in the sun must say to himself that nothing is done—nothing in actual fact—if he has not provided for the continuity of his effort and the relief of his post.

The concern of a teacher—as of anyone in authority worthy of the name—must be to search for and form his successor. Not with the care of the potentate who endows his offspring and makes barons of his preferred servants, but with that obsession for stability and continuity which are more necessary for education than for any other task. If no one after us follows our effort, the walls of this house without a roof will soon crumble!

The person who one day ceases wishing to enrich himself, to better himself on contact with nobler individuals, to cultivate and expand his mind, will neglect his task. This will constitute so many lost riches for these children. Even if he preserves them for himself, they will have made him better, and by that very fact, more capable and more worthy of inspiring these souls which are in his care.

Above all, he must never forget that a person can give only what he has. If he does not ceaselessly fill his mind, heart and soul with new seeds, he will very quickly be dried up and will no longer give forth anything good. If he does not wish to expend his youth in futile efforts, he must renew his riches and his enthusiasm at the pure sources of every richness and every gift: at the pure source of God and inspiring personalities who can guide him toward the excellent and the ideal.

THE PSYCHOLOGY
OF LITTLE GIRLS[13]

The young girl passes through stages that are completely analogous—at least until around the age of eleven—to those which we have just described for boys. But what characterizes her very early is a difference of rhythm, a time-lag in the evolution of the diverse mental functions which do not develop at the same ages as boys, and which especially manifest themselves according to different modalities.

Between birth and the age of seven, the study of differential psychology has not been brought very far by those who conduct it; neither are they always entirely agreed on the numerous imponderables which constitute the characteristics of this age. We will speak at length about the psychology of the third childhood, the school period, during which the differences appear between boys and girls. Between twelve and the end

[13] We thank Miss G. Taisne of *Service Central de Recherche et d'Action pour l'Enfance,* for the pertinent help which she so kindly rendered in the composition of this chapter.

of adolescence, there are less and less common lines between the two psychologies. For the study of this age we refer the reader to the various specialized works on the subject.

Before the age of six or seven

There are no fundamental differences between the psychology of boys and that of girls before the age of six or seven. But we very quickly observe a certain advance on the part of girls in the acquisition of the first automatisms, and above all in the initial manifestations of *social life*. In general, girls progress a month or two faster than boys. They rapidly acquire a more abundant vocabulary. Boys, once they have acquired the first usual words, seemingly seek to employ them more systematically and more personally than girls; by the use of "trial balloons" they probe the extension that any particular term may take and they verify its proper usage, whereas girls strive to assimilate other words. Around the age of four or five their repertoire is clearly more extensive than that of boys who exhibit a notable retardation of quantity to the profit of quality, the propriety of terms.

This example manifests one of the most basic and precocious traits of feminine psychology: a greater aptitude of social fusion, for adaptation to one's environment, a great suppleness for putting oneself in tune with one's surroundings.

Egocentrism regresses more quickly in girls, but this is not—as much as with boys—out of callous manifestations of opposition. In liberating themselves from this egocentrism they adapt themselves to their environment, conduct themselves "in accord" with it rather than "in opposition" to it. Their integration into the social sphere takes place more quickly, with less damage.

This ease of young girls in their environment is visible also in their games and their whole bodily comportment. Boys are in general more "clumsy" than girls, less voluble, less nimble and less adroit. This difference already visible in the progress of the three-year-old will appear with age and remain in the girl and the young lady in the rapidity of reflexes and the grace of movements.

Contrariwise, the two-year-old boy is already clearly more turbulent, more noisy, more callous than the two-year-old girl. Except possibly between six to eight years of age, the boy will always be more violent in his games. The four- or five-year-old girl will willingly use her shrewdness and her gracefulness; the boy of the same age will use his strength, his weight and his whole body.

Must we see in these differences that are already evident around the age of five a lesser need for physical relaxation on the part of girls than on the part of boys? This is a difficult question to resolve. What seems certain is merely that the excess of nervous energy is released in different ways. In boys, this release can only take place through the intermediary of muscle and movement, but in girls it is more often content with a less violent relaxation. In particular, fatigue resulting from focusing one's attention too long can in their case more easily evaporate in imaginative dreams which accompany calm games.

This is why, for example, a kindergarten teacher must often give boys rougher means of relaxing their nerves: although a round or a song will sometimes suffice to satisfy girls, boys will need races, shouting and tiring games. It is important to discern even from this age in girls a *tendency to be emotional* and in boys a tendency to be *muscular*. This difference will be accentuated even more in their future years.

However, we must not forget that between four and twelve children of the same sex exhibit great differences in character. Very often we have six-year-old girls ready for all the roughness of boys' games, and six-year-old boys attracted to the calm occupations of girls. Hence, we will often distinguish from the others the "big well-built girl" and the "little thin one."

Should we force these to practice the more normal occuptions of their companions? Should we let nature take its course? A science of character of the child would be very helpful in this case in enabling us to leave to each the freedom suitable for his development; at the same time, we would not deliberately ignore tendencies of character which might be full of consequences for the future and which could still be raised or limited during this period of formation.

Under the aspect of *intellectual development,* the differences are possibly less marked before the age of six than in the modes of playing that we have just mentioned. But already around the age of five we see the appearance of the greater richness of girls' imagination, the love of dreams, stories, appearances, the love to play comedy, to act out a personage ("I'll be the princess, and you say. . .").

By the "richness of imagination" we must understand the strong faculty of this age to place oneself in unreal situations; but we must not conclude from this to a great richness of invention, which remains quite limited until around the age of twelve, possibly even poorer and more traditional among girls than among boys.

The liveliness of these flights of the imagination—

resulting above all from a sensitivity already much more developed in girls—does not, however, exclude a very strict conformism, a return to traditional themes without any real grand invention. And when it does appear, invention remains part of the domain of the concrete detail: an action on the part of boys (a baroque action provokes the development of a new game: running while holding one foot), an object agreeably disposed on the part of girls (a rag becomes a dress, half a walnut becomes roast chicken, a cut and hollowed-out carrot becomes a pot of flowers).

We should also observe that the calmer girls' games permit them to achieve—more quickly than boys—a refinement of actions sufficing for delicate manual tasks when boys of the same age are still involved in global and violent corporal activities. This is one of the reasons for the greater precocity of girls in the learning process of writing and drawing.

The intellectual development of girls is thus dominated very much by the richness of their emotion, the vividness of their impressions, and the rapidity of their emotional reactions. While boys remain very slow in their reflection, girls react vigorously because of their intuition. In addition, this will be much truer during the age that follows.

The Fine Art of Teaching

There are girls endowed with a boy's temperament, and boys afflicted with a girl's temperament. Every child has a fine balance of masculinity and feminity. This balance varies constantly and becomes fixed only after puberty. It is most often futile to wish to straighten out nature.

But it is necessary never to close the normal way to these children, at all costs to treat with respect the reversals of balance which in the vicinity of the age of sixteen will yield a virile character to boys and feminine tastes to girls. May they never be catalogued as "tomboy" or "little girl"; jeers and even practical jokes would run the risk of accustoming them to consider themselves as such and the suggestion would have a dangerous role in this case.

Young girls should very quickly become aware of their real qualities as girls. For their emotional equilibrium it is necessary to give them a certain pride in the possibilities that are theirs, especially when a tendency erupts in them to envy boys and compete with them. This means in the long run to lavish on their gifts of speech, devotion, imagination and vivacity the same encouragement that the father lavishes on his sons' vigor.

For an analogous reason, it is dangerous to reprimand a child by comparing him to his sister or brother: "You see, at least he eats his carrots!" "You're not like your sister—you're always crying." "Be like your brother and keep quiet!"

Certainly, emulation can sometimes result. But very soon the child will become jealous of this other child who is always held up as a model for him. By reaction, he will maliciously take revenge on this "chowder head" and will tease him unmercifully; or he will assume a role of inferiority as proclaimed so loudly by everyone.

And why do you so fervently desire that this girl should be like her sister? I have more than a little impression that it is for reasons of convenience strictly personal to you.

From the age of seven to eleven

Until the age of six, the *social evolution* takes place in an analogous fashion in both boys and girls. However, it seems clear enough that girls who are already more flexible become a part of the diverse social spheres they frequent much more easily than boys.

From the intellectual point of view, this facility of fusion with one's environment allows a more rapid socialization of thought. We have said that young girls were more precocious in their acquisition of languages.

From the point of view of social relations, this fusion with one's surroundings explains why girls inflict less hurt on parents, manifest less violence in the jealousy of the older sisters for the newly arrived babies and experience less inferiority complexes. This is true until the age of six or seven.

Indeed, it seems that there is no longer the same relation once the seventh year is passed. Although Oedipal conflicts of the fourth year have been "liquidated" in general more easily in girls, it appears that around the age of seven a reversal of the situation takes place which is at times very delicate.

Until this age a more flexible character had spared girls the clashes with the paternal power which the boyish turbulence rendered obligatory. But toward the age of six or seven girls discover certain inferiorities in them which are at the origin of conflicts with the family environment.

Very often a more or less conscious deep regret arises in little girls at not being boys. This is termed the "refusal to accept one's sex," more or less tied to the pathological manifestations of the "castration complex" of psychoanalysts.

The source of these troubles can often be found in the blunders of parents. The father shows a boundless—and to tell the truth, not always justified—admiration for the exploits of his son and in addition the mother gives him greater freedom than her daughter.

Very often the child hears those close to her say: "Oh, you're only a girl" whereas she never hears anyone say to her brother: "Oh, you're only a boy!" Even more telling is the fact that when someone wants to reprimand a boy a little more harshly, he treats him like a "girl" and the boy regards this as a grave hurt.

This period is one of diverse failures which profoundly affect the sensitivity of girls. First of all, they lose the uncontested authority that they had up to now in the eyes of their brothers or neighborhood boys who reach the age of six-seven or eight.

They used to invent the games and give the boys a richness of detail which made the games they organized pleasant for all. Now boys of this age disdainfully refuse to let themselves be led by "girls" and desire the games of older boys: this represents the first defeat for girls.

The second defeat—which is just as frequent as and possibly even more serious—is that of girls in relation to their mothers who often surprise them in their dreams, inventions, embellishments of reality and playacting. The mothers—often harassed by the daily cares of the home—have "other fish to fry" rather than to listen to their daughters' nonsense. They send the girls on errands, make them peel potatoes; in short, they bring their daughters back to earth with a thud.

This would not be bad if such a return to earth were not brought about so callously at times. But the girls are rebuked sharply when they dream, they are accused of lying when they exaggerate a bit; their flights of imagination are turned into moral faults whereas the girls see nothing bad in them.

Such calls back to reality, performed by mothers without gentleness, rouse against them the hostilities of the Oedipus complex. The girls no longer feel confidence in them; they turn within themselves, and lose their assurance with adults as they have lost it with boys.

This results in a reversal of roles vis-à-vis those close to them. Since they are no longer as in the past the center of the family fascinated by their precocity, resourcefulness, enterprising spirit in organizing games, etc., they begin to assume an attitude of inferiority in the face of other children and adults.

But, whereas in the case of boys a feeling of inferiority was translated by a turning in on self and a surly isolation of self, in the girls' case it will manifest itself in a "search for approval" that is much more flexible. More anxious not to isolate themselves from their environment, they will be more concerned to find a good detour to achieve their purposes with children and adults.

In the presence of adults and especially their teachers they will seek to make themselves noticed, to obtain a favorite place by little attentions. Among their friends they will allot much more importance than boys to petty jealousies, jeers, quarantines, idle talk and prying.

Since girls have a more or less conscious feeling of inferiority toward boys because they can no longer interest them in their games, they will seek to embarrass boys, bother them and show up their immaturity. Frequently, in coed schools the girls will inhibit boys of the same age by their pointed sarcasms; while boys, less quick-witted, will answer clumsily with a punch.

Girls will very early delight in making boys react, take very lively interest in showing off before their eyes (in the same way that out of the desire for integration into the social environment they will seek to show off before their teachers and companions). However, seven- to twelve-year-old boys often treat such advances of "girls" with a sovereign contempt and go play with other boys. There is not yet between the two sexes the reciprocity of interest which will emerge at the approach of puberty. But there is already a certain rivalry of prestige, a growing concern for "what will they say?" between the two groups.

If the shock of starting school is less characteristic of girls than boys, it seems to be chiefly because of their more precocious and ever more lively desire not to isolate themselves, to find themselves in a sympathetic social atmosphere, to be able to be understood and loved, in order to expand themselves, gain confidence and develop their personalities.[14]

In this sense, the "crisis of the age of seven" can appear less violent in girls than in boys. But it remains more durable; it has reverberations even to the threshold of puberty in that vague insecurity which makes them seek the approval of those about them somewhat anxiously. The crisis of the age of seven seems to have a more profound effect on girls.

To round out the social evolution of girls less than eleven or twelve years old, we must note again a lesser propensity on their part for group activities. We encounter groups of girls less early, and they are clearly less numerous and less organized than among boys.

This in frequency probably results from the fact that girls are more subject to family chores, hence more

---

[14] The agreeableness of girls seems to rest for a longer time in inveigling dominance, and to be less quickly "oblative" than among boys. But later, beginning with the start of adolescence, the "oblativity" will in general be more clearly dominant in girls.

dependent on the mother. As regards the lesser cohesion of these bands and the limited number of girls
who make up each group, the reason seems to be found
in a less pronounced love for discipline and for collective undertakings.

Girls feel very little need for solidarity in groups
and correspondingly have a greater need for personal
affection. There will not be among girls—as there is
among boys—an all-powerful leader of the group,
armed with uncontested authority, ceaselessly enforcing
the cohesion of the group around herself by the whole
prestige of her cleverness and competence. Among girls
about ten years or so, we find instead little groups of
four or five friends quickly divided by jealousies, and
quickly "brought together again" by the medium of
neighborhoods and little conspiracies.

Viewed under the aspect of *character* and *moral
sense,* this social evolution is manifested by a lack of
simplicity and spontaneity; either girls "put on airs"
because they know someone is looking at them (coqu-
etry) or they take long detours to gain little advantages
or hide their silliness or defects.

If it happens that their social relations are bad
with those about them, their oppositions are expressed
more through a bad spirit than through blows, more
through jealousy and systematic disparagements than
through a violent opposition or indifferent scorn.

Boys willingly take one or other of extreme attitudes: flight or indifference, this will be clear. Girls will
not always manifest their opinion in the face of interest
but will gain revenge over their friends through a war
of needling and backbiting, passionately seeking to
uncover eccentricities and making artful use of scorn.

Their great sensitivity renders their feelings quite
versatile. Very susceptible, they will sometimes reverse

their attitude at the first blow to self-love. They eagerly persist in seizing the manias and passing weaknesses of those they no longer like.

Yet toward anyone who "knows how to take them by their good side" they show a heart much bigger than boys, seek more often to please by small attentions and help. Opening out to the gift of self, they love to be occupied with those weaker than themselves.

But this devotion conceals for a long time a compensation for their feeling of inferiority, a means of dominating at little cost and maneuvering their younger brothers as they are dominated by their mothers.

There are two ways open to children by which to compensate for a feeling of inferiority. They can lord it over smaller children: this can be done in a despotic fashion (superintend their pastimes, command their games or punish their foolishness); it can also be done in a maternal fashion (real help in difficult situations, protection against the cruelties of older children, etc.).

They can also lift themselves by their own bootstraps into the society of older children; if the child succeeds in taking part in their games, such an exploit will certainly increase his stature correspondingly (and often this is the proof of a solid psychical health).

Out of these diverse attitudes, boys generally choose the last; girls instead use the first two which manifest in the eyes of all, different temperaments: an unequal opening of the heart, un unequal social and emotional development.

While at the same age boys develop a love for fighting and chivalrous deeds, girls open out to sentiments of maternal love and relate to dolls a strength of feeling that they have been unable to lavish on little brothers at an earlier age.

The sentimentality of girls remains livelier and

more tender between the age of eight and eleven than boys of the same age. Girls are more given to caresses while boys tend to become more brusk. Less emancipated, girls remain more cajoling.

The intellectual development and school work of girls are also profoundly stamped by the influence of social behavior. Thus, as we have said, the richness of vocabulary is quite directly proportional to the ease of social relations. More abundant in girls at the beginning of language, the usual vocabulary seems clearly richer around seven or eight in boys. Girls recover their supremacy in this domain around ten or eleven and never lose it again.

The social difficulties of approximately seven-year-old girls renders them more conformist in language; whereas boys of this age will already search for the exact term that they want in order to express themselves, girls will use the words most common to their environment without any personal research of their own.

This conformism, or rather this flexibility of adaptation, is expressed in girls by a very clear advance in the school acquisitions around the age of six or seven. And during the whole of their school life they will dominate boys in matters of requiring adaptation, notably correct orthography. This advance in the ensemble of school life is rapidly attenuated around the age of nine and around ten or eleven fewer boys than girls will be behind in their classes.

Girls in general place more goodwill in conforming themselves to the passive discipline of school, except for making up by little slanders and jeers behind the teacher's back. If, externally at least, girls seem to integrate themselves better than boys in the school environment, it is doubtless because physically their need for corporal movement is less.

Thus, they have greater desire to be seen by the teacher, to gain her affection by little attentions, flowers and smiles. In girls there is not so much systematic opposition to teaching authority. In the case of boys, a teacher is often obliged to gain his prestige through a firm hand in order to be respected. In a girls' class there will generally be at the start a favorable presumption, and quickly enough ties of affection between teacher and students.

This facility of adaptation fosters the school successes of girls, both because of their desire to please the teacher (and consequently their interest is more easily captured and their effort is more enduring) and because of a love of learning that is often more lively; boys in general will not work as hard.

It is a mistake, and this is one of the ignorances of the coed school, not to take enough account in teaching methods of the fact that the intellectual receptivity in the school age child does not have the same form in the two sexes. First of all, the passivity of traditional methods—since it has different consequences in girls and boys—comes very close to being disastrous for both of them.

Physically, we have said, boys experience immobility more badly. But boys and girls often lose a great part of their natural curiosity in the repetition of the traditional schools; their imagination becomes impoverished before the rigidity of programs, and their energy turns elsewhere, toward the "things outside school" which more and more keep their minds outside the school walls while their bodies rest on the benches in class.

But let us also suppose that the interest of the students has been captured and their ardor oriented. One quickly notices that the results differ between boys and girls because the intellectual means are not the same. From the age of nine or ten onward the work of boys is imprinted with more logic and more realism. Confronted with any phenomenon whatever, they will seek the causes, the origins and the mechanical explanation.

Girls for their part, will take much better notice of actual modalities and appear more observant because they will go less farther to seek explanations. Boys will put more of themselves into their work which will reflect their personality; girls will take great care not to reveal themselves, but will manifest the sensorial richness of their language and the sensitivity of a temperament more capable of vibrating in unison with those around them. They will appreciate beauty, that which concerns the senses and that which evokes a sentiment, much better than the truth which concerns the reason.

Active teaching methods are very necessary to direct the lively imagination of girls toward the real, to limit the vagaries of the "imagination." Those girls who have been able to discipline their imagination and orient their curiosities have turned out to be more observant than boys because of their greater flexibility in the face of the data of reality.

It has been said with good reason that boys and girls approach scholastic differences with different attitudes; the former seek to conquer; the latter, to assimilate. Boys place more of their personality in their work, except for imposing by force their precise conception on the world about them which they are angry to discover is not in conformity with their idea. Boys apply themselves better to impartial observation, although often tinged with sentimentality.

The vocabulary itself expresses these differences: more precise, more technical and more abundant in objective terms in the case of boys, and more emotional, richer in sentimental colors, more charged with subjective opinions and consequently often less extended in girls.

It is necessary not to underestimate such differences of viewpoint and expression when reviewing the work of students. In a recitation, boys and girls can be rich in personality but each in his own way.

Girls will not dissect reality to seek therein the explanation of a structure, but to seek a source of new images. Utilizing less method in observation, they will utilize more finesse in the explanation. This will be possibly less sober and less precise than the approach of boys, but it will often be total in a more felicitous manner. Girls remain more global for a long time and less analytic.

If the imagination of boys at this age often remains in the intellectual domain, that of girls is already content with sentimental reverie. Girls long more for fairy tales. Boys will conjure up mechanical inventions, combats of complicated machinery, dream of fights, power and possession. Girls will prefer dreams surrounded by beautiful clothes, strange flowers, multicolored birds and prince charmings lost in love at their feet.

The Fine Art of Teaching

Sudden shifts of disposition, periods of boredom, inconstant efforts and bizarre character are very disagreeable but very normal between thirteen and fifteen years of age. It must not be forgotten that they are disagreeable even for the children who experience them.

Girls very quickly realize their defects, and are angered by them; but they remain as incapable of correcting them to the extent that these phenomena are deeply rooted in a physiological imbalance and remain so much less capable of fighting them to the extent that those around them multiply blunders and misunderstandings.

We can aid girls to retain their equilibrium only by showing an unshakable equality of disposition before this normal instability, by aiding at the right moment the slighest personal efforts, by patiently fostering the starts of energy and of self-mastery—yet not requiring prolonged efforts from these girls which would go beyond their possibilities.

The violent efforts to affirm their personality will often be expressed by excessive originality, peremptory declarations, boastful promises or excentricities lacking in the most rudimentary good taste. Petty oddities which girls themselves will laugh about tomorrow but which one would be wrong in challenging today.

The best remedy will always be to consolidate in girls what is worth saving and what makes up their personal value and to give them responsibilities corresponding to their capabilities, and by thus giving all their gifts the possibility of developing with the minimum of harm to themselves and those around them.

From the age of eleven to fifteen

The physiological and psychological turbulence of puberty is manifested in a more precocious way in girls than in boys of the same environment. Two years' advance is a normal mean in analogous conditions of climate, social class, habitat and family complex.

This mean, which is also very variable in time (between eleven and fifteen), is equally variable in intensity. Certain girls will pass this difficult age without apparent clash with their environment; others will present a crisis of opposition at that time which is often more violent than that of boys.

Physiological crisis, social crises of emancipation and opposition, moral and emotional crises, intellectual crisis—all of this will come and superimpose on, multiply and redouble the violence of conflicts as a direct result of the greater resonance of the nervous system.

The violence of these manifestations renders difficult and sometimes dangerous scholastic coeducation between the ages of eleven and eighteen, at an age when an instable will and the efflorescence of feelings that are often troubled and ambivalent multiply the obstacles confronting a healthy and balanced moral life.

There is much more to say about the characteristics of this age, the intellectual development, violent friendships, closed groups, dreams of love, interminable confidences, refusal of maternal authority, etc.

We prefer to refer the reader to specialized works published on the psychology of the adolescent. For we believe that it is much too vast a subject to be incorporated into our study which is not really concerned with adolescence but with school age.